SCOTNOTES
Number 17

Iain Banks' *The Wasp Factory, The Crow Road* and *Whit*

Alan MacGillivray

Association for Scottish Literary Studies 2001

Published by
Association for Scottish Literary Studies
c/o Department of Scottish History
University of Glasgow
9 University Gardens
Glasgow G12 8QH
www.asls.org.uk

First published 2001

A CIP catalogue for this title is available from the British Library

ISBN 0 948877 48 0

Subsidised by

THE SCOTTISH ARTS COUNCIL

Typeset by Roger Booth Associates, Hassocks, West Sussex

CONTENTS

SCOTNOTES

Study guides to major Scottish writers and literary texts

Produced by the Schools and Further Education Committee
of the Association for Scottish Literary Studies

EDITORS' FOREWORD

The *Scotnotes* booklets are a series of study guides to major Scottish writers and literary texts that are likely to be elements within literature courses. They are aimed at senior pupils in secondary schools and students in further education colleges and colleges of education. Each booklet in the series is written by a person who is not only an authority on the particular writer or text but also experienced in teaching at the relevant levels in schools or colleges. Furthermore, the editorial board, composed of members of the Schools and Further Education Committee of the Association for Scottish Literary Studies, considers the suitability of each booklet for the students in question.

For many years there has been a shortage of readily accessible critical notes for the general student of Scottish literature. *Scotnotes* has grown as a series to meet this need, and provides students with valuable aids to the understanding and appreciation of the key writers and major texts within the Scottish literary tradition.

Lorna Borrowman Smith
Ronald Renton

Section One
IAIN BANKS AND HIS WORK

The Author

Iain Menzies Banks was born in Dunfermline in 1954. His father was an Admiralty officer in the Rosyth Naval Dockyard and his mother was an ex-professional ice-skater. He was brought up in North Queensferry and later in Gourock on the Clyde. He attended schools in both towns before finishing his secondary education at Greenock High School and proceeding to Stirling University. After completing a degree in English Literature, with Philosophy and Psychology, he worked briefly for British Steel, part of the time at Nigg Bay in Easter Ross, and for IBM in Greenock, before moving to London in 1979. After finding success as a novelist, he moved back in 1988 to Scotland and his childhood home of North Queensferry, where he still lives.

Banks began writing seriously as a teenager, completing drafts of two (unpublished) novels while still at school. The first version of the novel later published as *Use of Weapons* was written at university; it was the starting-point for his later significant output as a writer of science fiction. Indeed, the novels, *Against a Dark Background*, *The Player of Games* and *Consider Phlebas*, and the novella, *The State of the Art*, were written in their first versions before Banks achieved spectacular success with his first published novel, *The Wasp Factory*, in 1984. It was the lack of success that he was having in getting his science fiction published that caused him to turn to writing fiction in realistic modern settings, what is often loosely and patronisingly called 'mainstream' fiction. Since *The Wasp Factory*, Banks has had no trouble in publishing any of his novels, and the pattern has been for him to produce a 'mainstream' novel and a science fiction novel alternately over the years since 1984.

His output has been remarkably productive and consistent. Up to the end of 2000, he has published ten mainstream novels and nine works of science fiction (including the novella, *The State of the Art,* with associated short stories). This is a large output for any novelist over a period of sixteen years, and it is certainly unusual for a Scottish writer in the modern era. Inevitably there have been accusations that Banks has written too much and that there has not been enough attention paid by him to ensuring quality rather than quantity. Some critics have suggested that there has been inadequate revising and editing before publication, with a resulting unevenness of style and expression. Banks himself has admitted that he does not spend much time on reworking what he has written. He tends to write a book over a period of two or three months each year, and spend much of the rest of the time on more pleasurable relaxing pursuits. This produces an apparent contradiction in that Banks, who has been dedicated to the writing profession from his childhood, nevertheless gives the impression that he does not take the actual business of writing too seriously. It would be quite wrong, however, to suppose that Banks is not a serious writer. Many of his books deal with and explore very serious issues, although not necessarily in a serious mood and style. Iain Banks has some very definite views about modern society and the prevailing philosophies that govern it, and in addressing these views in his mainstream novels, he can employ a dark sense of cruelty and violence as readily as a light humour and a relish for the pleasures of life.

The popularity of Iain Banks' novels was early established among a wide circle of readers. He has probably appealed most to readers of his own age and younger, who find themselves totally in tune with his contemporariness and the impression he gives of being immersed in the life of his generation. He can write knowledgeably about the world of rock music and drugs and fast cars, of student life and the street scene, of sexual relationships and business deals and family secrets. The realism of this kind of writing is, furthermore, counterbalanced by a vivid imaginative quality which infuses his mainstream novels no less than his science fiction with a sense of the fantastic and the surrealist possibilities of life. Whether Banks will always continue to have this appeal is open to question. As he approaches his fifties, he will inevitably be less in touch with the changing fashions of a receding younger generation. We can expect to see some changes in his novelistic persona over the next decade or two. For the moment, however, he seems to be content to come across as an amiable, relaxed personality, who is doing what he likes best, writing whatever he wants to for a receptive publisher and public; an image rather at odds with the capacity of his novels to shock and disturb as well as to entertain and amuse.

In recent years, there has been a growing development of some of his work into other kinds of media presentation. The novels, *The Bridge* and *The Wasp Factory*, have been adapted and produced for the stage. There was a successful BBC television serialisation of *The Crow Road*, which brought Banks' work to a wider audience. In 1999, *Complicity*, which has been seen as Banks' most shocking and violent novel, was released as a film. No doubt this is a trend that will continue, and we can expect to see more of Banks' work, perhaps including some of his science fiction, appearing on the screen in years to come.

The Work

(a) *The Mainstream Novels of Iain Banks.*
As already mentioned, the first novel that Banks published was *The Wasp Factory* (1984). When it appeared, it was greeted by a great deal of both favourable and hostile criticism. The extracts from reviews printed at the beginning of the paperback edition give some sense of the divided and extreme nature of the comments the novel attracted. Words like 'brilliant', 'power', 'polished', 'exceptional' and 'masterpiece' are contrasted with 'sick', 'obscenity', 'sadistic', 'preposterous' and 'repulsive'. It is not a book that the reader can just accept with passive placidity. An extreme reaction of either admiration or revulsion is more probable. On the face of it, the story of an adolescent who tortures and executes living creatures, who describes the murder of three young relatives, and who has a brother committed to an institution for setting fire to dogs is not likely to be the average person's idea of a good read. Yet, as time has passed since the original publication, and as the author has gone on to consolidate a high literary reputation with many later novels, it is possible to see that behind the sensationalism of *The Wasp Factory* there was a skilled handling of a serious theme and a clever use of well-established literary devices to create both a good story and a sound commercial prospect. A later section will examine the novel in detail and consider its real qualities free of any prejudice against its surface features.

The following year, 1985, saw the publication of *Walking on Glass*. This novel, set in London, where Banks was at the time working in an office, has a structure of three apparently separate narratives running in parallel throughout the book. The first, on the level of everyday reality, is the story of an art student, Graham Park, and his love for and unsatisfactory relationship with Sara ffitch. The second narrative, on the level of distorted reality, is the story of Steven Grout, a severely paranoid schizophrenic, told through events on the day he is sacked from his job up to the accident that leaves him passive and brain-damaged in an enclosed mental unit. The third narrative, on the level of apparent fantasy, shows two old people, Quiss and Ajayi, playing a succession of obscure board games in a great crumbling Gothic castle set in the winter landscape of a dying planet. The walls are of fossilised books and the floors and ceilings are of glass; hence the title of the novel. The structure of the novel is cleverly devised so that the reader holds these three stories separate in the mind as they are read concurrently, but comes to realise at the end that they are in fact connected and are to be understood consecutively. Grout's street accident is observed near the end of the Park narrative, and Ajayi and Quiss are seen at the end of the Grout narrative as two old patients obsessively playing board games with incomplete sets in the library of the mental home. Thus the novel is one in which the structure is an element fully as important as the plot, and in which imagination is used to heighten realism into surrealism and fantasy.

The fascination with complex structure and the blending of reality and fantasy is carried further in Banks' next novel, *The Bridge* (1986), which he has often referred to as his favourite among all the novels he has written. A whole book could be written about *The Bridge* and its complex, subtle and superbly imaginative story of the anonymous Scottish engineer and his life in the Edinburgh of the nineteen sixties, seventies and eighties, paralleled by his mental life while in a coma after a car accident on the Forth Road Bridge. In his coma life, he is an incomer to the life of the Bridge, a great inhabited structure spanning the sea between the City and the Kingdom, in an invented fantasy world. Another dimension to the story is to be found in the dreams that the protagonist, known as Orr in his coma life, either experiences or invents for his psycho-analyst on the Bridge. Thus the story of *The Bridge* moves on three levels: a coherent chronological level of reality in a real Scotland experienced and observed by the anonymous engineer, whose name is withheld directly by Banks but revealed indirectly through clues embedded in the story; a coherent level of fantasy within the created and symbolic world of the Bridge, which nevertheless owes its conception to the real Forth Rail Bridge in whose massive shadow Banks spent some of his childhood, linking the City of Edinburgh with the Kingdom of Fife; and a level of fragmentary and apparently incoherent dream and invention drawn from literary and psychological sources. The range of cultural, literary and popular reference on all levels of the story is very wide, making *The Bridge* a very difficult yet rich book to read; a full set of accompanying notes would be required for the serious reader who wishes to pick up all the possibilities of the text as they are presented.

1987 saw the publication of *Espedair Street,* a novel in which Iain Banks examines the world of rock music and the cult of the pop hero. The story of Danny Weir, songwriter and performer, traces the rise of the Scottish rock band, Frozen Gold, from its small beginnings in the West of Scotland to the height of international success and fan adulation, and then through tragedy to a final break-up. Known as 'Weird' from the way his name appears in the school class register – Weir.D – Danny Weir goes from a poor childhood in Ferguslie Park in Paisley through a wealthy life-style marked by excessive behaviour and drug-taking to a solitary hermit-like existence in a disused church in Glasgow before he finally seeks happiness with a girl he had known in Paisley in his youth. The novel has many apparent points of contact with real events and personalities in the music world, but Banks keeps his story fresh, individual and entertaining throughout without any of the sensationalism that attracted criticism to *The Wasp Factory.*

However, in *Canal Dreams* (1989), Banks produces a story that many readers might find distasteful. Hisako Onoda, a Japanese cellist with an international reputation who, nevertheless, has a phobia about flying, is held up on her voyage to a tour of Europe by an outbreak of guerrilla warfare in Central America which traps the oil-tanker she is sailing on in one of the lakes of the Panama Canal. In this state of artificial suspension she remembers her childhood, has a love affair with one of the ship's officers, and has a succession of dreams, some of them disturbing and violent. The action comes to a head when the ship is taken over by a gang of guerrillas who murder the passengers and crew, and rape and torture Hisako. The violence of her dreams and memories fuses with the violence of her real situation, and she becomes imbued with the spirit of revenge. The climax of the novel comes as she works out her vengeance, destroying the guerrillas, their vessel and the tanker itself, with its cargo of oil. Banks is undoubtedly writing sensationally on the theme of rape-revenge that was briefly fashionable in films and stories. The result is a disturbing novel which, although skilful and well-told, seems to aim at a mass readership with a taste for violent action and cruelty; there is almost a potential 18-rated film lurking behind the pages. Banks himself seems to regard *Canal Dreams* as one of his least satisfying works, remote in location and spirit from the world he knows at first hand.

With *The Crow Road* (1992) and again with *Whit* (1995), Iain Banks is operating with greater confidence in more familiar territory. Later sections in this guide will examine these novels. However, it is worth noting that both of them use Scottish settings and characters, and demonstrate a lighter touch in the action and style. Although there are serious issues raised in the novels, Banks lets his natural wit and sense of humour have full opportunity to play freely with the subject matter. The results are much more satisfying than the strained effects of *Canal Dreams*.

Complicity (1993) saw Iain Banks returning to the territory of violence and apparent sensationalism. The plot, which revolves around a series of sadistic murders and attacks on prominent members of the Establishment, that is, the ruling elite of politics, law and business, seems to be a vehicle for Iain Banks' feelings of hatred and disgust for the selfish and materialistic right-wing trends he observed in British public life through the Eighties and Nineties. There is a lot of reference to contemporary events: indeed, the main character, a hard drinking, heavy-smoking and drug-taking Edinburgh journalist, has been deeply affected by the death and destruction he observed during the Gulf War. The corruption he sees all around and his keenness to expose some of it makes him the target of a malicious plot, so that he is even suspected of being the 'Radical Equaliser' who is committing the murders. It has been argued that in *Complicity* Banks has gone too far by letting personal feelings destroy artistic detachment and outraging good taste by portraying sexual excess and cruelty so explicitly. Banks himself has said that there was a deliberate intention on his part to show critics that he had not put the tone of *The Wasp Factory* totally behind him and that he could outdo it if he wished. *Complicity* has appealed to readers widely, despite, or perhaps because of, its sensational aspects, and has been the first of Banks' novels to be adapted into a film.

A Song of Stone (1997) seems at first sight to be a slighter piece of writing than Banks' previous novels, and to be closer to some of his science fiction. The story concerns the last members of an aristocratic family, Abel and his sister Morgan, between whom there exists an incestuous love, and the castle they inhabit with their servants at a time of social collapse and civil war. Their castle, the 'song of stone' of the title, is taken over by a band of irregular soldiers under the command of a woman lieutenant, and the story is then worked out in terms of the relationship between Abel and Morgan and Loot, the lieutenant, with an inevitable progress towards death and destruction. Although the story is left unlocalised in precise terms, the natural and social descriptions suggest a Scottish setting, poised between Lowlands and Highlands, in a possible post-disaster near-future. Iain Banks is clearly trying something different from his other mainstream novels, a more surrealist narrative revisiting some themes first touched on in *The Bridge* and *Canal Dreams*.

Iain Banks' most recent novel, at the time of writing, has been *The Business* (1999). The central idea of the plot, that there exists a vast international organisation which has carried on its commercial business over many centuries since the days of the Roman Empire and still wields great unseen power in influencing politics and business throughout the world, recalls the idea of the Culture, which is at the centre of much of Banks' science fiction. But, whereas the Culture seeks to influence less developed societies and civilisations indirectly for their own good, using its massive technological superiority, the Business is actuated by more human desires for profit and influence and has to rely on more fallible agents and methods, thus opening up the possibilities for corruption and selfish ambition. When one of the Business's highly placed executives, Kate Telman, discovers such corruption in action, she is faced by a conflict between her sense of morality and her loyalty to the Business. In contrast to *A Song of Stone*, the action ranges widely and quickly over a worldwide scene, from Glasgow to the Himalayas.

The range of novels covered here, illustrating the varied and prolific achievement of Iain Banks over sixteen years, shows clearly that there is a powerful and imaginative writing talent at work, with no sign of slackening. And this is only one side of Banks' literary output. The science fiction novels, which remain to be briefly considered, would in themselves be a considerable body of writing for any one novelist.

(b) *The Science Fiction of Iain M. Banks*
It was science fiction that Iain Banks first set out seriously to write. As already mentioned, the first versions of four of his science fiction novels existed before he broke into print with *The Wasp Factory*. An interesting quirk of publication history has ensured that the Banks of the mainstream novels is easily distinguished from the SF Banks. His first publisher, Macmillan, thought that his middle initial, which he wanted to use for *The Wasp Factory*, was rather fussy and recommended that it be dropped. Subsequently, Banks put it back for the science fiction

novels (he had actually considered using a complete pseudonym, but decided not to), so that there is a slight distinction being created between mainstream writing and science fiction, but not a significant one. However, his publishers have consistently created a visual difference between the two genres by publishing the mainstream novels in elaborately designed black and white covers, and the science fiction with colourfully illustrated futuristic covers. Iain Banks has always left open the possibility that the initial M could be reinstated for all his novels, but this seems unlikely as there is a strong commercial angle now to be considered in any change.

The core of Banks' science fiction is the concept of the Culture. It forms the context for six (to date) novels and one novella; two other non-Culture novels were written by Banks deliberately as a digression from his main theme to see if he could in fact do without the Culture as a narrative element. So any consideration of Banks' science fiction has to start with this invented universe of the Culture, Banks' powerful and coherent realm of the imagination within which most of his SF narratives are developed. Fortunately, Banks has written a long and developed account of the Culture as an aid to his many admirers and fans ("A Few Notes on the Culture": Sf-Lovers Archives, Rutgers University, 1994, accessible on the Internet). A few points extracted from these notes would probably be helpful.

> "Firstly, and most importantly: the Culture doesn't really exist. It's only a story. It only exists in my mind and the minds of the people who've read about it....."
>
> "The Culture is a group-civilisation formed from seven or eight humanoid species, space-living elements of which established a loose federation approximately nine thousand years ago. The ships and habitats which formed the original alliance required each others' support to pursue and maintain their independence from the political power structures – principally those of mature nation states and autonomous commercial concerns – they had evolved from....."
>
> "The Culture, in its history and its on-going form, is an expression of the idea that the nature of space itself determines the type of civilisations that will thrive there. The thought processes of a tribe, a clan, a country or a nation-state are essentially two-

dimensional, and the nature of their power depends on the same flatness. Territory is all-important; resources, living-space, lines of communication; all are determined by the nature of the plane (that the plane is in fact a sphere is irrelevant here); that surface, and the fact the species concerned are bound to it during their evolution, determines the mind-set of a ground-living species. The mind-set of an aquatic or avian species is, of course, rather different. Essentially, the contention is that our currently dominant power systems cannot long survive in space; beyond a certain technological level a degree of anarchy is arguably inevitable and anyway preferable. To survive in space, ships/habitats must be self-sufficient, or very nearly so; the hold of the state (or the corporation) over them therefore becomes tenuous if the desires of the inhabitants conflict sufficiently with the requirements of the controlling body......."

"(Going along with this) is the argument that the nature of life in space (with its vulnerability) would mean that while ships and habitats might more easily become independent from each other..... their crew – or inhabitants – would always be aware of their reliance on each other, and on the technology which allowed them to live in space...... The mutuality of dependence involved in an environment which is inherently hostile would necessitate an internal social coherence which would contrast with the external casualness typifying the relations between such ships/habitats. Succinctly; socialism within, anarchy without."

"The Culture ..... has gone beyond (both the market economy and the planned economy) to an economy so much a part of society it is hardly worthy of a separate definition, and which is limited only by imagination, philosophy (and manners), and the idea of minimally wasteful elegance; a kind of galactic ecological awareness allied to a desire to create beauty and goodness."

"There is another force at work in the Culture aside from the nature of its human inhabitants and the limitations and opportunities presented by life in space, and that is Artificial Intelligence. This is taken for granted in the Culture stories, and – unlike FTL (faster than light) travel – is not only likely in the future of our own species, but probably

> inevitable....... Culture starships – that is, all classes
> of ship above interplanetary – are sentient; their
> Minds (sophisticated AIs working largely in
> hyperspace to take advantage of the higher
> lightspeed there) bear the same relation to the fabric
> of the ship as a human brain does to the human
> body; the Mind is the important bit, and the rest is a
> life-support and transport system. Humans... are
> unnecessary for the running of the starships, and
> have a status somewhere between passengers, pets
> and parasites."

From these few quotations from a long survey of the Culture
articulating and clarifying the basic principles and features of
Banks' science fiction universe, it can be seen that Banks has
approached the writing of his novels in this genre with a
commitment to creating a coherent context for his stories. He has
not been content to accept some of the lazy conventions of popular
science fiction, with what he sees as inbuilt political assumptions,
many of them the product of American Cold-War stereotypes
about democracy versus totalitarianism, Right versus Left,
human emotions versus machine logic, Doctor McCoy versus Mr
Spock. The result is that the political and philosophical thrust of
his writing is Left-leaning, opposed to traditional authority
attitudes and sentimental leanings towards the social patterns of
the past. Equally, in Banks' writing there is no deference towards
religious beliefs and practices which prevent a full acceptance of
the need for the fullest possible development of science and
technology as the best way forward for the human species.

So, in the Culture novels, the people of the Culture are seen as
carefree, long-living, pleasure-seeking, egalitarian in attitudes,
and fully integrated with the non-human intelligences (the Minds
of the starships and the 'drones' who perform lesser functions)
with whom they share their society as partners, not in any
master/servant relationship. Such a world would not seem to be
the kind that would produce dramatic events or strong story-
plots; it is indeed from the relationships between the Culture and
external forces and civilisations that the stories of Banks' science
fiction arise. The basic dilemma for the Culture is the question of
how far it is justified in becoming involved with socially and
technologically less advanced societies with a view to reforming
and 'civilising' them. An explicit and open involvement is the way
of imperialism, something repugnant to the Culture philosophy; a
hidden and indirect involvement is the way that is chosen,

necessarily a shifty and questionable compromise. So the typical heroes and heroines of the novels are characters on the borders of the Culture, hired mercenaries or agents with unconventional Culture backgrounds, who may be given a mission or an assignment to 'intervene' and influence events in another society to bring about an outcome beneficial to both that society and to the Culture. They are 'James Bond' figures up to a point, flawed and violent, but kept to their duty by a Control figure, often a strong, dominant and sexually powerful woman agent of the Culture. It would be true to say, therefore, that Banks' science fiction grafts a tale of action and violence, with rather conventional spy fiction features, on to his complex and imaginative basic concept. This is particularly true of the first three of his Culture novels: *Consider Phlebas*, *The Player of Games* and *Use of Weapons*, as well as the novella, *The State of the Art*. However, two of the most recent novels in this group, *Excessions* and *Inversions*, show some significant variations on the theme. The latest science fiction novel by Banks is *Look to Windward*, the title of which suggests a link with his first, *Consider Phlebas*, since both titles are phrases to be found adjacent to each other in the 'Death by Water' section of T.S. Eliot's long poem, "The Waste Land".

Two novels that are not dependent on the notion of the Culture, *Against a Dark Background* and *Feersum Endjinn*, show clearly how Banks does not need this underlying concept to create interesting and strongly imagined science fiction. *Against a Dark Background* is a straightforward story of quest and pursuit, in which a group of friends rally round one of Banks' strong female protagonists to seek an awesomely powerful lost weapon and find it before being caught by a pursuing group from a fanatical religious sect with revenge on their minds. The theme of a conflict between a saving technology and destructive superstition is strong in the novel. In *Feersum Endjinn*, the idea of rediscovering a lost super-science in order to save the future of the human species in the face of a threatened cosmic disaster is central to the plot.

The relevance of Banks' science fiction to his mainstream novels is not hard to find. In the science fiction, some of Banks' central preoccupations about life and society are made explicit, clearly brought out in a kind of fiction that is shaped to highlight the issues: the need for rational and humane policies to be promoted in both personal life and social organisation; the need to embrace scientific and technological development as the only way forward to a better life for all; strong political and philosophical dislikes, amounting to a revulsion against backward-looking and anti-humane conservative attitudes and religious superstitions that are often used to justify behaving with cruelty and discriminatory prejudice towards other individuals and social groups. In Banks' mainstream novels, these attitudes are often present, but modified and tempered by the needs of a realistic story and coherent credible characters.

Three Chosen Novels for Study

The novels that will be discussed in the following sections have been chosen because of their quality as stories that entertain the reader and as extended fictions that use important ideas and themes as elements that give depth and power to the events portrayed. *The Wasp Factory* is not only a sensational and savagely humorous story, but a thought-provoking study of a misdirected personality. *The Crow Road* is a long and complex story of a family with its secrets, but is also a portrayal of a young man's quest for self-knowledge and love, aspects that contributed greatly to the novel's success as a television drama. *Whit* deals with a similar sort of quest by a young woman, and contains a highly developed study of how religion operates on people at different levels of personal and social life. In these three novels, Iain Banks can be seen in his most characteristic literary moods, from the humorous sensationalism and shock treatment of *The Wasp Factory* to the more natural and appealing everyday realism of *The Crow Road* and *Whit*.

Section Two
THE WASP FACTORY (1984)

When Iain Banks' first published novel appeared, it attracted an exceptional amount of attention. The newspaper critics were totally divided in their reactions: some of them condemned the novel as a sick piece of sensational exploitation, making a joke out of cruelty and the sadistic torturing of animals, with no real literary merit whatsoever; and others hailed it as a brilliant first novel, presenting a very skilful picture of obsession and psychological disturbance, and satirising the genre of horror writing with a biting humour. Readers have to make up their own minds about this disagreement. Probably most thoughtful readers would come down somewhere between these two extremes, recognising the novel's real merits as a fascinating study of a surrealistic family, while still having some concerns about how far good taste is being rejected. Yet, despite the mixed reception that the novel received, there is no doubt that it has been highly popular over the years since then and is well established as a classic of its kind, a darkly comic piece of modern Scottish Gothic fiction, drawing on well-known elements of the horror story and of fantasy and placing them skilfully in a modern situation.

Synopsis of the novel

The action of *The Wasp Factory* is spread over twelve days, each of which is dealt with in a separate chapter.

1. *Day One (Wednesday)*
The Sacrifice Poles. Frank Cauldhame and his father learn from the local policeman that Frank's elder brother Eric has escaped from the mental hospital where he has been kept secure. Frank has been going his rounds of the sites where he displays the corpses of creatures he has killed and has already had a warning from 'the Factory' that something special was going to happen. The odd circumstances of Frank's lonely life in the traditional family house on the island near the town of Porteneil are suggested, along with the curious habits of his father and Frank's own physical appearance. A secret is hinted at, involving his father's locked study, which Frank is keen to see inside. The day ends with a telephone call from Eric, revealing that he is going to

return home. There is the clear suggestion that Eric is very
unstable and violent; he has apparently been committed to the
hospital for setting fire to dogs.

2. *Day Two (Thursday)*

The Snake Park. Frank completes the rounds of his Sacrifice
Poles. He remembers how Eric's mother had died in giving birth,
so that Eric was in a way responsible for her death; he had also
suffered from migraines all his life, and thus his instability may
have had both a psychological and a physical cause. In his
fantasy play, Frank had been intending to have a War, but Eric's
impending return home would make that difficult. Instead he
sets about constructing a dam system, and after lunch, when his
father has gone off to Town, he conducts a massacre of rabbits
with his air rifle, bombs and flame-thrower. He also tries the door
of his father's study, but finds it securely locked as usual. Frank
remembers the deaths of three of his uncles from accident and
suicide. Principally, however, he remembers how he had
murdered his cousin Blyth by putting a poisonous adder inside
his artificial leg, the first murder he had committed when still
only five. It is revealed that, within the next three years, Frank
went on to murder his young brother Paul and another cousin
Esmerelda.

3. *Day Three (Friday)*

In the Bunker. Frank admits his hatred of Women. In the early
morning he goes through his careful washing and dressing ritual,
before going out to survey his territory. He visits the tree that
used to be his large catapult, the Killer, with which he would fire
stones and small animals to a considerable distance. He then
visits the old gun emplacement, the Bunker, where he lights a
candle in the skull of Old Saul, who had been a family pet dog,
and incinerates a few wasps. In the afternoon, Frank goes into the
nearby town of Porteneil to buy a new catapult and airgun pellets,
and visits the local cafe, but does not meet any of his
acquaintances. He returns home to make some new bomb tubes; it
is revealed that the cellar of the house is full of cordite, an
explosive that has to be kept dry to prevent it from becoming
unstable. After having dinner and some home-brewed beer with
his father, Frank goes to his room to work on his war-maps and to
bring his records of the weapons in his secret stores up to date.
The day ends with a telephone call from Eric. Frank keeps this a
secret from his father. Eric has become more violent and

threatening in his language, claiming to be cooking and eating dogs, and ending his call by smashing up the callbox and telephone.

4. *Day Four (Saturday)*

The Bomb Circle. In the morning Frank tries out his new catapult and goes for a run along the shore of the island. He ends up at the Bomb Circle, and remembers how he had killed his young brother Paul by persuading him to bang on the sides of an unexploded Second World War German bomb until it went off and blew him to pieces. In the evening Frank goes drinking in the Cauldhame Arms with his friend Jamie the dwarf. Jamie sits on Frank's shoulders while they talk. Frank has told Jamie about Eric's escape and likely return home. Later in the evening, they meet up with two girls while dancing to a punk rock band, but Frank is too drunk to enjoy the company. He is on the point of vomiting, and is desperate to urinate after all his pints of beer. It becomes apparent to the reader that Frank has some physical problem about using a male toilet, but the matter is not explained. Eventually Frank relieves himself completely behind a petrol pump and Jamie takes him back to his house, where he is kindly received by Jamie's mother. Later he makes his way home to bed along the shore by the sea, remembering how once he had seen the reflections of gas-flares from the oil rigs far out in the North Sea.

5. *Day Five (Sunday)*

A Bunch of Flowers. Frank spends most of Sunday in bed recovering from his Saturday night out. He remembers all the circumstances surrounding the death of his little cousin Esmerelda, whom he had murdered by tying her to a large home-made kite and letting the strong wind carry her away out to sea. Frank's father reveals that he had had a phone call on the Saturday evening, which he thought was Frank playing a joke; Frank realises it must have been Eric. On Sunday evening Eric calls again. Frank intercepts the call and pretends to be talking to Jamie since his father is listening; this infuriates Eric, who again becomes violent and smashes up the phone booth. Frank comes to the conclusion that he will have to work some kind of magic to deal with the problem of Eric, probably using the skull of Old Saul, who was "the root cause of everything". First, however, he would have to consult the Wasp Factory.

6. *Day Six (Monday)*

The Skull Grounds. This is a chapter of reminiscence, in which part of the dreadful family secret is revealed. Frank's hippy mother, Agnes, who had deserted him at birth, returned to the family home to give birth to another child, Paul, who would be Frank's half-brother. While Agnes was in labour, the family dog, Old Saul, savaged young Frank, mutilating and apparently biting off his genitals. In revenge, Frank's father strangled the dog to death just as the baby was born. Agnes waited only two days before deserting her husband and children again, breaking her husband's leg with her motorbike when he tried to stop her. Frank's father refused to let doctors into the house, set his leg himself leaving him with a limp, removed Frank's genitals from Old Saul's stomach and buried the dog near the house in what Frank later came to call the Skull Grounds. Ten years later, Frank recovered Old Saul's skull and set it up in the Bunker as a powerful object of worship. So Frank's secret apparently is that he has been castrated by the bite of Old Saul and left to grow up as a psychologically damaged eunuch. We learn in the following chapter that Frank spends Monday repairing and improving the Wasp Factory, which we have not yet been introduced to in the story. Eric does not call in the evening.

7. *Day Seven (Tuesday)*

Space Invaders. Frank spends the morning with Jamie in the Cauldhame Arms drinking and playing Space Invaders. In the afternoon he prepares the Wasp Factory for use the following day, catching a fresh wasp to act as its trigger and sacrifice. He then goes to his dam across the stream, completes it and blows it up with one of his bombs. In bed that night he meditates on the power of the Wasp Factory, which is now revealed to be an elaborate device for foretelling the future, Frank's modern advance on the traditional methods of reading the omens.

8. *Day Eight (Wednesday)*

The Wasp Factory. Frank rises early, takes his sacrificial wasp, and goes to the loft where the Wasp Factory awaits him. It is a large construction built round an old clock-face that had once hung outside a bank in Porteneil; there are twelve exits from the large clock-face each leading to a different and unpleasant mode of death for the wasp used as the sacrificial victim and inserted through the glass cover on to the clock-face. By observing the movements and fate of the wasp, Frank feels able to draw conclusions about what the future has in store. In this case, there is no delay. The wasp moves quickly towards the exit leading to Death by Fire, and Frank directs its burning by means of a lighter over a pool of petrol. Frank interprets the meaning of the event as a warning of a future involving Eric and a destructive fire, and feels he has to confirm it with a visit to Old Saul's skull in the Bunker. As he concentrates intently with one hand on the skull containing a lighted candle, trying to focus on Eric and his physical nature in order to establish some kind of communication, he experiences a profound physical sensation like a violent explosion of fire which throws him back from the skull. Frank sees this as proof that Eric's mental state is too strong and violent for him to communicate and that he is bent on destruction when he returns home. Frank goes home and spends the rest of the day in the house. In the evening, while his father is out, Frank has another phone call from Eric. Eric sounds dangerously calm, and reveals that he is not in a call box, but in a holiday cottage that he has broken into; it becomes clear that he is not very far away.

9. *Day Nine (Thursday)*
What Happened to Eric. In the morning, after visiting Jamie at his home, Frank goes with his pack on his back for a walk in the hills behind Porteneil. In the beautiful surroundings, he thinks about Eric and the way in which his life had been destroyed. In childhood, Eric had been bright, sensitive and intelligent with a good life in prospect for him. He had been close to Frank, who had hero-worshipped him, and they had played a lot together when Eric was home on holiday. There was a darker side, however, for Eric suffered greatly from migraines and had a fixation about death. Yet he had decided to study to be a doctor, and did well at university for two years. At a time when his migraines were particularly bad and he had been rejected by a girl he loved, Eric was helping out in a large hospital with the care of greatly handicapped children and had an experience with one child one night that was so traumatic and disturbing that it caused a breakdown, which, although he seemed to recover, completely changed his attitude to life. He neglected his studies, started drinking and taking drugs, and set fire to his books, so that eventually he had to return home. He paid no more heed to Frank, and became violent and threatening to the local children. The end came when he started catching dogs and setting fire to them. He was certified insane and committed to a succession of institutions until at last he was put into a long-term secure hospital. Now he

has escaped and is on his way home. Frank scans the landscape
with his binoculars, feeling that Eric is not very far away, but sees
nothing and returns home for the evening.

10. *Day Ten (Friday)*
Running Dog. Thinking again about Eric, Frank wonders if part of
his problem has arisen from having too much of a feminine side,
and from having a father who had had strange ideas about the
bringing up of children. Frank blames his father for some of what
has happened. In the morning, Frank goes for another scouting
excursion round the approaches to the island, across the sand-
dunes and towards the town dump. He sees nothing on his walk,
but when he comes to a large holiday bungalow standing empty, he
hears an animal screaming in pain. It turns out to be a dog that
has been set on fire. Frank follows it and kills it with his catapult
to put it out of its misery. Convinced that this is Eric's work, Frank
returns home. In the evening he has a call from Eric who seems to
be surprised to be accused of the torture of the dog, and denies it.

11. *Day Eleven (Saturday)*
The Prodigal. It is a hot day, and Frank spends a quiet morning
checking the Wasp Factory, the Bunker and the Sacrifice Poles,
and doing some target practice with his catapult and knife. After
dinner, in the afternoon, he goes out to keep watch through his
binoculars, and sees his father, who appears to be drunk, heading
into town. Going back to the house, Frank finds that the telephone
is off the hook and deduces that his father has taken a call from
Eric. He settles down in the house to wait for Eric to arrive, but
receives a call, seemingly from his father, saying that Eric has
been captured and asking Frank to go into town and meet him at
the library. Frank sets off but on the way finds that the telephone
wires have been cut. Suspecting a trick either by his father or by
Eric, he goes back to the house and continues to keep a look-out.
However, he falls asleep and when he wakes up, hears somebody
else in the house. It is his father, very drunk, who eventually goes
to his room and passes out. Frank finds the keys for the study and
goes at last into this secret sanctum. What he finds shocks him,
although he does not yet understand. There are his infant
genitals in a jar of alcohol, and packages of male hormones in a
box in a drawer, along with other items that Frank cannot see the
purpose of. He goes to confront his father with this evidence, but
before he can find out anything, Eric mounts his attack. A flock of
blazing sheep are being driven towards the house setting fire to

everything in their way, and Eric is breaking into the cellar containing the explosive cordite, intent on setting it off. Frank manages to stop him and Eric runs off just as the shed containing Frank's bombs goes up in a set of violent explosions. However, the house is saved. As things fall quiet, Frank demands an explanation from his father. It is revealed that the supposed genitals of Frank in the jar are in fact only plasticine. Frank's father at last reveals the truth.

12. *Day Twelve (Sunday)*
What Happened to Me. On the morning of the next day, Frank goes out into the fresh morning while his father is trying to explain things to the local policeman and finds Eric lying peacefully asleep. He takes his brother's head on his lap and sits reviewing what he has been told and how it has totally changed his outlook and perception of himself. He is in fact not a boy, but a girl; Frances Lesley, not Francis Leslie Cauldhame. Her father had been responsible for a massive deception, seeing the mutilation of his daughter by Old Saul as an opportunity to conduct a bizarre experiment in sex development, feeding the little girl male hormones to restrain the female physical development and direct Frances towards a male orientation. So she grew older, never able to grow into a full adult, to be either properly male or female, scarred both physically and psychologically. The violence and the murders were an attempt to make up in aggressive male behaviour for the suppression of her natural instincts and impulses. Like the trapped wasp in the Wasp Factory, her path and fate were being determined by forces she could not control. Now, however, there is the chance that some of the damage can be undone and Frances can begin to live a more normal life as the woman she is intended to be.

Structure of the novel

The synopsis of the novel plot shows that the basic element of construction is a sequence of twelve days over which the main action takes place. From internal evidence, this is revealed to be from a Wednesday to a Sunday. This is a useful way of keeping the action moving on at a steady pace. It brings a certain degree of inevitability into the atmosphere of the novel: whatever Frank might wish or try to do on one level about the approaching arrival of Eric back at the Cauldhame house or on a deeper level about the shape and nature of his life, he is at the mercy of time which keeps moving on steadily. Just as the great clock face dominates the Wasp Factory giving it the quality of an impartial Fate ruling the victims within its power, so Time rules the creatures subject to it and their fate will be worked out whatever choices of path they make. "Each of us, in our own personal Factory, may believe we have stumbled down one corridor, and that our fate is sealed and certain (dream or nightmare, humdrum or bizarre, good or bad), but a word, a glance, a slip – anything can change that, alter it entirely, and our marble hall becomes a gutter, or our rat-maze a golden path. Our destination is the same in the end, but our journey – part chosen, part determined – is different for us all, and changes even as we live and grow." (WF, pp.183-184) As the days pass, Frank is moving inevitably towards the resolution of both the Eric problem, which is uppermost in his mind, and his own personal problem in life, of which he is only dimly aware. It is appropriate that, after the hectic and surrealistic events of the final Saturday, the final mood is of a Sunday or Sabbath peace in which Frank can feel that a start can be made to a new sequence of days in which the terms of living will be greatly changed, hopefully for the better.

A simple progression of events from one day to the next is not, however, strong enough as a plot structure to maintain dramatic interest or tension. The element that Banks uses to give a sense of approaching menace, to suggest movement towards a climax of violence, is the sequence of telephone calls made by Eric to the house, calls which Frank tries to conceal from his father, pretending they are from his friend Jamie. The irrational violence that is already within Eric is intensified by Frank's pretences and finds an outlet in the smashing by Eric of the telephone and the callbox he is using, thus increasing the sense in the reader that when Eric finally appears, there will be real harm done. Add to this the awareness from what Eric is saying that he is getting nearer to home with every call, and the sequence of telephone calls can be seen as an important device for adding atmosphere to the narrative and giving unity to the structure.

In many of Banks' later novels, he makes use of parallel narratives, that is, the regular switching from the main line of the story in the present to another sequence of events, usually in the past, and back again, thus keeping the reader's attention engaged on more than one aspect of the novel's total story. In a novel like *The Crow Road*, it can become very complex; however, in *The Wasp Factory*, the story line is relatively simple. The story switching that Banks uses is confined to a movement between the present events involving Frank on the twelve days of the novel's action and the events in his past that have a bearing on the kind of person he is now, the story of his family members and the murders he has committed of some of them. Thus, in each chapter there is an element of reminiscence by Frank of past events in his life. For example, in Chapter 1 Frank recalls (to inform the reader) the curious circumstances of his upbringing and childhood as a deliberate policy of his father to keep him isolated; Frank has no official existence, no papers, no school attendance, no medical records; the reason for this is only revealed at the end of the novel. One or two chapters are mostly given over to recollection of the past; Chapter 5 is primarily a recounting of the circumstances of the death of cousin Esmerelda. However, it is the case that there is comparatively little digression throughout the novel from the main plot, unlike most of the later novels of Iain Banks.

In terms of structure, therefore, *The Wasp Factory* has a generally straightforward linear pattern, moving chronologically through the events of the twelve days, with a build-up of tension as the climax of Eric's arrival home and the revelation of Frank's real nature is approached, concluded by a brief final chapter of calm reflection on what has occurred.

Characters of the novel

Note: To avoid awkwardness in referring to Frank as either male or female, the male pronouns 'he', 'him', 'his' and 'himself' will be used throughout, except when dealing with Frank's condition after he finds out the truth about his gender.

Frank. As the first-person narrator, Frank is the main focus of character interest. Everything in the narrative comes to us through his consciousness, and he is revealed to the reader both by what he tells us directly about himself and by what he does. Yet, as he reveals more and more about himself and his upbringing, and learns his true nature, the reader's view of him changes and the judgement of him formed early on in the novel is altered radically.

In the early chapters, the impression gained of Frank by the average reader is of a very sick-minded adolescent living an unnaturally lonely life and wrapped up in a fantasy world of cruel war-games and the sadistic torturing of defenceless creatures. The area surrounding the isolated family house on its island linked to the mainland by a narrow bridge has been divided up mentally by Frank into a landscape inspired by the reading of

action fantasies of the Swords and Sorcery genre. There are the
Sacrifice Poles, the Bunker (a kind of underground temple), the
Rabbit Grounds, the Snake Park, the Bomb Circle, Kite Pyre Dell
and the Skull Grounds. Each of these locations has a violent
significance within Frank's personal history, being areas
associated with the killing of people or animals, and he moves
through these places like the aggressive macho hero of the
fantasy stories. He has his stock of powerful weapons, and his
ritual practices that are needed to maintain the fantasy world
intact; in particular, the Wasp Factory, an elaborate apparatus for
foretelling the future through the sacrifice of wasps to the random
workings of the killing machine. So he wages his imaginary wars
and makes his sacrifices as if living in the male-dominated world
of Conan the Barbarian. The element that is lacking is the sexual
fantasy, for Frank reveals that he hates Women. They are rather
too close to him for comfort; there seems to be a degree of fear in
Frank's attitude to them.

In parallel to the fantasy world that Frank has created, there
is the real world that he has to find a place within. The
Cauldhames are an old family belonging to the North-East of
Scotland, living in their traditional family house close to the town
of Porteneil on the Moray Firth. Frank and his father live alone,
with only an elderly housekeeper, Mrs Clamp, who comes in every
day to cook and clean. Mr Cauldhame seems to have a number of
eccentric obsessive habits, which he indulges at the expense of
Frank, who has no official life outside the house and has been in
effect educated by his father instead of at a school. By now,
however, any formal education has finished and Frank is left to
his own devices almost completely. His only friend outside the
home is a dwarf called Jamie, whom he meets in Porteneil, where
they regularly drink and play Space Invaders together. Frank
enjoys the companionship of Jamie and confides in him about Eric
and his father up to a point, but still remains basically withdrawn
from outside contacts. The only other friend that Frank has had is
his elder brother Eric, whom he has only known during Eric's
holidays from private schools and university up until the time
when Eric was committed to a mental hospital. Eric had been a
hero-figure for Frank and had taken a close interest in him up
until the point when he began to become seriously disturbed in his
mind and emotions.

It is not therefore surprising that Frank should have grown up
into adolescence as a solitary being, living out a set of violent
fantasies drawn from his reading and from television and video

games. Suspicious of his father's attitude towards him, cut off by his father from the genuine and normal social contacts of school and friends, separated from his brother and the rest of his family, he has not acquired the natural and desirable experience of real life that would regulate and limit the violence of his fantasies and put them into their proper perspective as harmless elements in his imaginative development.

Yet it becomes clear even from the first chapter that there is something else about Frank that acts as a powerful inhibiting factor in his engagement with life. It is something physical, with understandable accompanying psychological hang-ups. The reader learns from a succession of references, which are seemingly explained in Chapter Six, that Frank believes he has been seriously mutilated by the bite of the family dog, Old Saul, and has lost his male genitals; he is a eunuch, castrated and impotent, and feels inadequate in performing any specifically male role, whether it be urinating in a male toilet or having social contacts with girls. So he makes efforts to over-compensate for this inadequacy, in taking strenuous physical exercise, drinking many pints of beer, and, most questionably, working out his violent macho 'heroic exploits' on helpless creatures, insects like wasps, and rabbits and other small mammals, the victims of his extreme male desire to dominate and subdue. There is a strong feeling of resentment suppressed within him, which finds its most destructive outlets in the killing of the weakest and closest members of his own family, cousins Blyth and Esmerelda and younger half-brother Paul.

The feelings of the reader about Frank and his activities become less and less hostile as more is revealed about Frank and his problems. It is not a feeling that his actions are excusable, but a realisation that Frank is in fact a victim himself and that his violence is a kind of bewildered and pathetic reaction to the situation he is in, one for which he bears no responsibility; he is lashing out in revenge at the wrong targets. It is only when the true physical nature of Frank's situation is discovered that the true cause and originator are revealed, the target he ought to have been aiming at.

The truth about Frank, of course, is that 'he' is not an aggressively male sadist, nor an impotent eunuch, but a physiologically and psychologically retarded young woman. She is the subject of an odd and unethical experiment by her scientist father, who appears to be a prey to a disturbed complex of feelings towards women, aroused by the two main women in his life, the wife who died in childbirth, and the wife who deserted

him twice and crippled him. Frank has been prevented from
arriving at a normal stage of puberty through the regular doses
of male hormones and bromide that her father administers to her
food: the hormones to discourage the physical characteristics
that are female and to encourage those that are male, and the
bromide to suppress sexual feelings. All that is abnormal or
warped about Frank is, therefore, the unforeseen by-product of a
deliberate policy by her closest relative. The final chapter, in
which Frank realises and begins to come to terms with her
damaging sexual misdirection, is the beginning of hope for
Frank, when she can cease to be an unwitting victim and can
begin to take responsibility for her own life, difficult though that
will certainly be.

In spite of the severe obstacles that seem to prevent us from
identifying with Frank, whether we are seeing him as sadistic
killer, disabled eunuch or gender-disorientated experimental
subject, it remains the case that Frank comes across to us as a
strong character, for whom it is impossible not to feel liking and
sympathy. He is articulate, observant, taking a positive relish in
all his doings however distasteful or unpleasant they may appear
to us. This may point to a possible weakness in the conception of
Frank and his situation. Would such a strong thoughtful
adolescent be so passive in accepting the restrictions of his life
with his father in an isolated house, cut off from normal social
contacts? The fact that he is permanently under the influence of
drugs administered by his father does not adequately explain this,
given that he is so physically active and mentally alert. Perhaps
we can accept its possibility in a younger Frank, but it would be
reasonable for us to see the existing situation as being incapable
of lasting much longer. Just as Frank's father seems to be aware
that Frank's female nature may be liable to manifest itself
suddenly despite all his male hormones, so we can see the escape
and approach of Eric as heralding a necessary and unavoidable
change in Frank's life that cannot be any longer delayed. Frank is
already probing into the mystery of his life, seeking the key to the
study that holds the solution, the clues to the truth. With or
without the crisis of Eric's arrival, Frank is bound to find out.

Father. Frank's father, Mr Cauldhame, is given no individual
name in the story and has no narrative viewpoint of his own. That
is, he is presented to the reader only through Frank's point of
view, and we have to decide for ourselves what his motives were
for the the way he has chosen to bring up his sons, Eric and
Frank. As Frank presents him to us in the narrative, Father

seems to be a curious obsessive figure, with his eccentric passion for having everything in the house measured and labelled. Yet he is a highly educated man, a specialist in chemistry, or more probably biochemistry, who has chosen to give up an academic career in a university to live on his family money in the ancestral home and devote himself to his own studies and the upbringing of his younger child. He has educated Frank personally, giving him in some ways a better formal education than he would have received at school. This could be seen as showing a high sense of his responsibilities as a father. However, on the other hand, there seems to be a streak of irresponsibility in the way that he has behaved. Frank has no official existence; his birth was not registered and he has none of the documents that are necessary for full functioning in modern society and the Welfare State. Frank believes that this is an outcome of his father's hippy-anarchist youth in the '60s, and that his father may now be regretting this rash decision. He is also to some extent playfully irresponsible in the way that he has fed the young Frank false information about some things as part of his education; it is possible, nevertheless, to see this as a deliberate educational technique designed to make Frank cautious about accepting uncritically what he is told by 'authority'. On the evidence of the information given to the reader early in the novel, it is possible to see Father as a well-meaning but eccentric man, concerned about his son but trapped by his earlier irresponsibility in a difficult legal situation concerning Frank's official status. But it becomes clear that actually he is a more important figure in the story, whose influence on Frank is crucial and positively damaging. His role in *The Wasp Factory* must be seen as a dual one, as father (with all the associations of authority that paternalism carries) and as scientist (with the associations of the irresponsible use of knowledge and power).

In his forties, tall and slim with a slight stoop, with a delicate womanish face and dark eyes, plus a bad limp and a drinking habit, Father does not seem like a typical caricature of 'the mad scientist'. Yet that is how he seems to be presented to the reader. It appears that he is conducting some kind of private experiment in the way he is bringing up Frank. This involves the use of hormones and drugs administered to Frank in his food without his knowledge, spying on his movements, particularly his drinking in the local pub, and an elaborate web of deceit about Frank's past and his mutilation by Old Saul as a baby, involving the keeping of a fake set of infant male genitals in a jar in his locked study as a clinching piece of proof if necessary. By no stretch of the imagination can these actions be seen as those of a responsible and caring parent; Father has apparently reduced his own son to the status of a laboratory subject, an animal kept for scientific purposes and observation. Yet the motives cannot be entirely those of the dispassionate scientist, the searcher after new knowledge. Some private hang-up, a personal psychological problem, seems to be lurking in the background. Frank seems to glimpse this at the end of the story; "My father dressing Eric up as a girl was just, as it turned out, a rehearsal for me. When Old Saul savaged me, my father saw it as an ideal opportunity for a little experiment, and a way of lessening – perhaps removing entirely – the influence of the female around him as I grew up" (p.181). It may, however, be more subtle than Frank suspects. The dressing up of his son Eric in girl's clothes for a short period of his childhood before he went away to private school could be seen as an attempt by his father to retain some sense of the female in his life after the death of his first wife, Eric's mother, in childbirth to lessen the sense of loss. On the other hand, the prolonged attempt to make his daughter, Frank, into a boy is clearly a conscious reaction against the double desertion of him by his second wife, Agnes, her betrayal of him with another man leading to the birth of her second son, Paul, and her crippling of him with her motorbike. It is a rejection of femininity by scientific means, regardless of the physical and psychological effects on the innocent Frank. The guilt of her father is never fully admitted by Frank even at the end. The last sighting of Father by Frank in the story is of him trying to explain things to the local policeman. The final legal result of his actions, if indeed they all come out into the open, is never considered.

Eric. For most of the novel, Frank's elder brother Eric is an absent character, brought to us only as someone remembered by Frank from his childhood as a lost companion and friend. This positive likeable Eric has changed terribly and is now a threat steadily approaching to disrupt the lives of Frank and his father. He is an angry irrational voice on the telephone posing some kind of menace to his own family, although this is never made specific. It is only in Chapter 11 that he actually comes on the scene as a kind of returned prodigal son, with destruction as his purpose, trying to set fire to the house and blow it up with the cordite in the cellar. In the last chapter he is at peace sleeping with his head in his sister's lap. What will happen to him is not discussed but it can only be a return to a secure institution.

What has caused Eric to become so mentally disturbed is made very explicit by Frank in his reminiscence. From the moment of his traumatic birth, when the pressure of his large head caused both the haemorrhage that killed his mother and the cranial distortion that gave rise to his own chronic migraines, Eric seems to be under a curse. The death of his wife in childbirth certainly gave rise to Mr Cauldhame's feeling of alienation from his son, causing him first to dress Eric in girl's clothes and later to pack him off to a boarding school out of the way. His development to manhood largely away from the presence of his father, first at school and later at university, seemed to have produced a brilliant outgoing likeable personality, darkened only by the recurring migraines. Yet a combination of personal and study problems brought Eric to the point where a single appalling experience in the hospital where he was helping out, the discovery of the maggots consuming the brain of the severely handicapped baby, was enough to tip him over the edge into a downward spiral of neglect of his studies, drugtaking, aggressive behaviour and finally the psychotic cruelty of setting fire to dogs. The extent to which Eric has focused on his father and home as being to blame is not made clear, but his intention in returning home after escaping from the institution is clearly to take some kind of revenge. Frank remains the one person with whom he can communicate, even though his tones over the telephone to his younger 'brother' are violent and abusive.

We are clearly intended to see Eric as being another victim of the Cauldhame family situation even though he is much less subject to his father's eccentric theories and actions. The future outlook for him is no brighter than it is for Frank.

Themes in the novel

Father and Son
The two main characters of the novel, Frank and his father, are locked together in one of the most powerful relationships within literature and social life. The tension between father and son has been extensively explored in many kinds of writing, notably in fiction, in biography and autobiography, and in drama. Scottish writing has been particularly concerned with this theme, and some of the most significant Scottish novels and stories deal, partly at least, with the strong feelings and conflicts between a usually dominating father and a developing and maturing son. This has been seen by some critics as being linked with the

powerful position of the Presbyterian Church within Scottish society for more than three centuries. Its strong Calvinist doctrine of an authoritarian God laying down an uncompromising set of laws to His children became the model for family life, and the heavy remote father of the Victorian age became a familiar figure in reality and in literature.

In *The Wasp Factory*, Frank's father cannot be seen as heavy and religious; yet he carries with him the weight of scientific authority, is the dominant influence in Frank's upbringing and is working out a hidden system of control of Frank regardless of Frank's wishes and real interests. While there is no open conflict between father and 'son', Frank is sufficiently sensitive and intelligent to be aware that all is not well and that his father is keeping some great secret from him. There is therefore an undercurrent of suspicion and tension between the two characters that is not totally resolved even at the end when all is revealed. This father-son relationship is the most important of the novel, beside which the Frank-Eric relationship is of less significance.

The Misuse of Science

Throughout the modern age, there has been a major social debate about the place of science and technology in human life and the dangers of their misuse, even their perversion, in ways that are opposed to natural human development. It has already been made clear that Iain Banks is firmly on the side of science and technology as necessary and desirable additions to life, being the main allies of humanity against the things that limit its potential happiness, security and capacity for further development. However, that is not to say that Banks would condone the flagrant unethical misuse of science against individual or collective human interests. So, while Frank's father may be potentially worthy and admirable as a skilled scientific specialist, he is to be condemned for going astray and perverting the powers of science for his own selfish ends in violation of Frank's basic human rights.

The first major literary treatment of this theme was Mary Shelley's novel, *Frankenstein*, now regarded as a major classic of horror, which examined the ethics of trying to create life by scientific means. The scientist Frankenstein creates a living being from the body parts of people who have died, but despite some initial success, the intelligent and self-aware being degenerates and becomes embittered and violent (giving rise to the popular misconception of it as being a 'monster', the subject of many a lurid horror film treatment). It is clear that Banks had this literary forerunner of his novel in his mind when writing *The Wasp Factory*: the choice of the name 'Frank' may be a clue; so also may be the location of the action in an isolated old house, rather like the popular presentation of Frankenstein's laboratory as being remote from other human dwellings in a crumbling castle or mill. Frank's father is not, of course, creating life from scratch using body parts, but he is essentially creating another human being from a living original, using hormones and drugs to alter the true nature of his own child. He is 'playing God' in much the same way that Frankenstein was accused of doing. In the transformation of Frank into a violent, sadistic killer of animals and murderer of his own close kin, we can see the same kind of degeneration of a being from a psychologically healthy condition into a state of bitterness and futile impotence. Frank is not aware of the causes of his condition, as Frankenstein's monster is, but the effects on him are the same.

Dual Personality

Linked to this theme of the misuse of science and technology is the popular Scottish literary theme of dual or split personality. The notion that two or more different personalities may inhabit one human body is both a traditional one going back through generations in stories of possession by the Devil or evil spirits and a modern one deriving from theories and case-studies of psychological disorders displaying schizophrenic or multiple personality behaviour within one individual. In Scottish literature, the novel, *The Confessions of a Justified Sinner*, by James Hogg and the novella, *The Strange Case of Doctor Jekyll and Mister Hyde*, by Robert Louis Stevenson blend the traditional and the psychological aspects into two classics of their kind. In *The Confessions of a Justified Sinner*, a young man, Robert Wringhim, who is repressed and warped by an extreme religious upbringing, is haunted and possessed by a mysterious Devil-figure who can take the shape of Robert and others and acts as the projection of an evil side to Robert that is at odds with Robert's better nature. So Robert acts out through this other personality the feelings of resentment and the desire for revenge that are suppressed within his real self. There are some parallels here with Frank in *The Wasp Factory*. Frank too is warped by his upbringing, although the causes are physiological, and so another Frank takes possession of his body expressing a violent and revengeful side to Frank stimulated by his maltreatment.

Perhaps *The Strange Case of Doctor Jekyll and Mister Hyde* is more directly applicable to *The Wasp Factory*. The basically good but occasionally sinning society doctor Henry Jekyll is able to use his scientific knowledge to create a drug that changes his nature, even his physical appearance, so that he becomes Edward Hyde, a being without any moral scruples of any kind, a completely natural and debased creature who delights in cruelty and violence. At first Jekyll relishes the freedom that this gives him to express the darker side of his real nature. But through excessive use of the drug and an inability to continue making it, Jekyll becomes imprisoned in the personality of Hyde and his good nature is lost. In *The Wasp Factory*, the scientific side of Jekyll is paralleled in Frank's father with his scientific curiosity allied to a selfish personal impulse; he creates the cocktail of hormones that changes Frank's physical nature and appearance from Frances to Francis. The 'Mister Hyde' that Frank becomes delights in cruelty practised on the innocent, and he seems to have no moral reservations about what he does. The 'Dr Jekyll' side is kept permanently suppressed until the end, when Frank has the chance to rediscover her true lost personality. Thus *The Wasp Factory* is more optimistic in its conclusion than *Jekyll and Hyde*. Unlike Stevenson in his more serious work, Banks, against all the evidence at times, is fundamentally an optimist about humanity and its situation.

The humour of the novel

The discussion of the novel so far has focused on very serious aspects of the story and characters. It is necessary here to point out that, despite the horrific nature of so much of the content on the surface and the thought-provoking nature of the underlying themes, *The Wasp Factory* is a novel containing a great deal of humour. There is a long-established tradition of humour that finds its subject-matter in horrific events and situations that in real life would be too serious to laugh at. Irvine Welsh's novel, *Trainspotting*, has a lot of this kind of humour, as do many films, and many war novelists have relied on it to make their stories more bearable. Often in the past called 'black humour' or 'gallows humour', it involves joking about death and suffering. Iain Banks, in *The Wasp Factory*, makes use of this in his own individual way.

The most noticeable technique is probably that of humorous reduction. The cruelties practised by Frank are unpleasant in reality, whatever their scale, but in the context of literature, reading about the massacring of wasps, gerbils, hamsters, mice, even rabbits, using the elaborate weaponry that Frank has created, takes on a touch of the ludicrous and slightly ridiculous. A climax to the novel that involves a flock of blazing sheep cannot be taken with real seriousness and a feeling of humanitarian indignation. Even the murders of young children by such methods as inserting an adder into an artificial leg, banging on the side of an unexploded bomb, and ensuring the victim is carried out to sea by an enormous kite must arouse more of a smile than a shudder. By this means of placing the horror in a context of farcical humour, it is removed to a certain distance from the reader and filtered through an emotion that is not the normal one for reacting to what is grim and unpleasant. To serious-minded people, this may seem a gross lapse of good taste, but Banks is clearly not wanting readers to react to the story in a serious-minded way. There is a possibility that he is directing his story to readers, probably quite young, who have been brought up to some extent with an awareness of comics and cartoons in which the violence is stylised and exaggerated for immediate effect, often humorous, so that there is no lingering tendency to analyse it in the terms of real-life violence.

Another technique, at first sight closely related to humorous reduction, is that of humorous exaggeration. The deeds of Frank, their locations on the island, and the weapons that he uses, are thought of by him in terms of literary fantasy. As he plays his war games and carries out his slaughters, he thinks of himself as if he were the barbarian hero of a Swords and Sorcery adventure of the type made popular in action comics, in pulp fiction and, more recently, in computer games. Just as such a hero would have personalised, even personified, his steed and his weapons with their own special names, so Frank has his steed, the bicycle Gravel, his trowel Stoutstroke, his catapult Black Destroyer, the Killer tree catapult, his War Bag and Head Bag. He has christened the scenes of his deeds with their own evocative names, like the Sacrifice Poles, the Bomb Circle, the Snake Park, Kite Pyre Dell, and the Rabbit Grounds. His temple is the Bunker, and, of course, there is his sacrificial altar of prophecy, the Wasp Factory. The mock-heroic tone that this gives to his story is one that many writers of the past have created for the purposes of humour and satire; making fun of the most serious literary forms of the day has always been a popular literary technique. *Don Quixote* was a parody of romances about knights and their battles with monsters and enchanters; *Gulliver's Travels* was a satire on society that imitated fashionable books of travel and exploration;

and the contemporary writer, Terry Pratchett, is using stories and themes of serious literature and culture for humorous purposes. So Iain Banks is again appealing to a certain type of reader, who is aware of the whole fashion for popular violent epic fantasy, by making Frank into a self-aware teenager who goes through his daily life working out a humorous continuous parody of his favourite reading matter. It amuses Frank, and on another level it amuses the readers.

Of course, the humour lies more in the tone than the actual events of the story and cannot be sustained as the real circumstances of Frank are revealed. The sense of Eric's inevitable arrival and the reasons for his madness break through the black comedy atmosphere, and Frank's individual tone of voice, which has been observant and self-analysing throughout, takes on a deeply serious edge as she ponders what has happened to her and what she can do now with her life.

Section Three
THE CROW ROAD (1991)

Talking in an interview for the magazine *Midweek* (7/5/92) about his recently published novel, *The Crow Road*, Iain Banks said: "I thought I'd try and write a family saga, but a wacky, weird and zany family saga, as is my wont! It's very much like *Espedair Street* and *The Wasp Factory*, in that, although it has fantastic elements, it's still meant to be grounded in reality. In a way the first line is an overture – you read it and think, well, this can't be reality – and in fact it is. You get to the end of the chapter and there's a completely rational explanation for it. Throughout the book Prentice is bemoaning the fact that reality isn't weird enough, and the magic's gone, and he's surrounded by complete nonsense. Weird shit is happening all around him, and gradually he comes to realise that. I think it's what an objective reader of my books would expect from a family saga I'd written. This is as normal as it ever gets."

The Crow Road has turned out to be one of Banks' most popular novels. Set firmly in Scotland, and spanning two generations of three related families, it focuses mainly on the attempts of the young Prentice McHoan to unravel the mystery of the disappearance of his favourite uncle Rory McHoan eight years before. The first sentence, "It was the day my grandmother exploded", as suggested by Banks, sets the tone of apparent fantasy which is finally seen to be reality. *The Crow Road*, like many another large family saga, contains other stories within it: a detective story, a love story, a story of father-son conflict, and a full measure of both comedy and tragedy. It is not surprising that *The Crow Road* was the first of Banks' novels to be adapted for the screen. A successful television version of it in four parts was shown during the 1990s.

The settings of the novel

After the exotic Central American setting of *Canal Dreams*, Iain Banks returned home to Scotland for the setting of his family saga of *The Crow Road*. The title has a specific Scottish association, with a particular street in Glasgow which Banks makes use of for a small part of the action. However, the Glasgow Crow Road running from Partick to Anniesland is not the main association in the title. More important is the use of the phrase, "The Crow Road", or "C.R.", as the title of a folder containing notes by one of the characters for a proposed book. Even more important is the traditional meaning of the expression, "the crow road", as the road that leads to death, a doomed path, a phrase that has an almost folklore quality and one which is of especial significance in a novel which has death as a major element in both the past and present action.

The principal setting of the action is an area of Argyll, between the Sound of Jura and Loch Fyne, containing three important locations for the story: the imaginary town of Gallanach (on Inner Loch Crinan), where the Gallanach Glass Works, owned by the Urvill family, is situated and where the Watt family live; Gaineamh Castle (near the ancient Celtic fort of Dunadd), restored by Fergus Urvill, and now his family home, containing an observatory; and Lochgair (a real place on the shore of Loch Fyne), where the McHoan family live. As he has done in other novels, and as many other writers have done also, Banks has blended real locations with invented ones. The landscape is real, with its hills and lochs, but it contains unfamiliar features. The town of Gallanach, with its factory, pubs and council estate, its derelict docks and its great Ballast Mound, is a Banks invention; so too is the railway that runs down Loch Fyne through Lochgair and on to Gallanach.

The other main setting of the action is Glasgow, where Prentice is a university student, living in a flat in Grant Street, and later in a large town house flat in Park Terrace. It is when he visits his Uncle Rory's former girl friend, Janice Rae, in her flat in Crow Road that he acquires significant information about his Uncle Rory that leads eventually to the solution of the mystery of his disappearance.

By his variety of setting for the events of the novel, Banks makes it clear that he is dealing with a more representative Scotland than that found in the pages of many previous Scottish novels that are rooted firmly within a small community, whether it be a small town, a rural farming district or a city slum. This intention to look at a wider spectrum of Scottish life is reinforced by Banks' choice of three loosely-related families as the central elements in his story.

A saga of three families

The story of *The Crow Road* apparently deals with three families: the McHoans, a middle-class family living in a large house in Lochgair and associated over two or three generations with the management of the Gallanach Glass Works; the Urvills, a prosperous family owning the glass works and a local country estate; and the Watts, a working-class family living in a council house in Gallanach. The families belong to different social classes, but are loosely related to each other through marriage, so that on family occasions, such as the funeral of Prentice's grandmother Margot McHoan, they are likely to meet up and renew acquaintance. Physically too, they live in the same area of Argyll within a few miles of each other and so they are likely to maintain contact with each other. In fact, the families keep up an institution of an occasional Family Sunday, on which the Urvills and the McHoans take turns in playing host to each other, plus the family of Bob and Louise Watt. In a sense, therefore, the three families could be said to represent a single extended family, within which the main action and themes of the novel are worked out. The family trees that follow should make clear how the different branches of the 'family' are interconnected.

Family trees
(Major characters of the novel are identified in bold type.)

McHOAN FAMILY

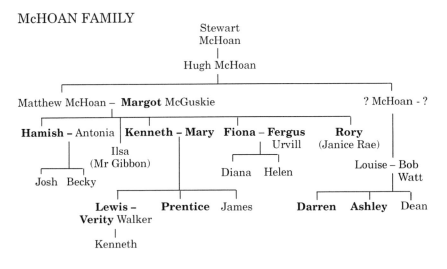

Family trees (cont.)

URVILL FAMILY

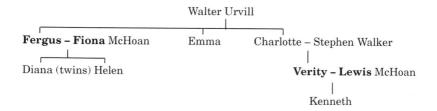

Walter Urvill

Fergus – Fiona McHoan   Emma   Charlotte – Stephen Walker

Diana (twins) Helen

Verity – Lewis McHoan

Kenneth

WATT FAMILY

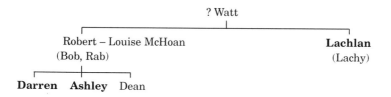

? Watt

Robert – Louise McHoan   **Lachlan**
(Bob, Rab)   (Lachy)

Darren   Ashley   Dean

The structure of the novel

We saw in Banks' first novel, *The Wasp Factory*, a basically simple structure, or pattern of the story. The main action followed the events of a series of days from beginning to end, with the hero Frank Cauldhame acting as the narrator. The narrative was in the first person, with everything seen through the consciousness of Frank. Within this main narrative, the present time of the action, there were memories of past events which built up into a secondary narrative that filled out and clarified the events of the main narrative. This is a very common novel pattern. Hardly any serious novel deals only with a succession of events in the present, and the first-person narrator is one of the commonest features of story-telling.

In the novels that have followed *The Wasp Factory*, Iain Banks has shown an ability to experiment and vary his novel structures.

However, the switching from a main present narrative to a secondary narrative of the past has remained central to his novel planning. In his novel, *The Bridge*, it has taken the form of a switching between an apparent fantasy world and the real world; however, the fantasy world turns out to be the 'present' consciousness of a man in a coma, and the events of the real world are those of his own past. In *The Crow Road*, Iain Banks has produced the most complex and at times the most puzzling structure of any of his novels, either before or after. Yet basically there is the same distinction between main and secondary narrative, between the past and the present. The main narrative is always recognisable by being in the first person, with the "I" representing the consciousness of Prentice McHoan. The secondary narrative, or narratives, are in the third person of an imagined observer or the consciousness of one of the principal characters.

The story of the novel

(a) *The narratives*
Banks has said of the novel: "I was pleased with it in the end, even though structurally it's all over the place, a rag-bag of a thing." It is certainly difficult to make a brief synopsis of *The Crow Road*, since the narrative is so complex and divided up through the eighteen chapters of the novel. In every chapter there is narrative of the present, containing within it narrative of the past, 'flashbacks' to perhaps more than one particular period of time. Essentially there are four main narratives, covering a time-span of nearly fifty years, from about 1945 down to March 1991. The earliest narrative, covering events from 1945 to 1981, is presented from the third-person viewpoints of Prentice's father, Kenneth McHoan, and his younger brother Rory. The next narrative in sequence is the narrative in fictional form of family events during 1979-80, written by Rory and preserved on computer disks. Events of the years 1980 to November 1989 are recalled by Prentice but are presented in the third person as the next identifiable narrative. The primary narrative, however, is the first-person account by Prentice of the events of November 1989 to March 1991, happening 'now' in the present of the novel time, the period in which all the previous family events and mysteries are resolved. The clearest way of summarising the novel will be to deal with each of these narratives in order.

(b) *1945-1980: Kenneth and Rory*

The earliest events of the story concern Kenneth McHoan, Fergus Urvill and Lachlan Watt as young boys with their sisters playing hide-and-seek in the ruined Gaineamh Castle in Argyll just as the Second World War is drawing to an end. Kenneth is revealed as observant and thoughtful, emotionally affected by the natural surroundings and the ruined castle; Lachy is aggressive and foulmouthed; and Fergus is refined and repressed. Later the three boys go to Fergus's parents' large house and have tea in his room surrounded by his possessions, including a glass display case containing his museum of archaeological finds. Lachy is clearly jealous of Fergus and his obvious privileges, and taunts him to the point where Fergus loses control and smashes Lachy's head down through the glass case. Lachy loses an eye, and Fergus's father has to pay compensation to his family as well as supplying him with a glass eye from the family glass works. In this episode the class jealousy felt by the working-class Lachy Watt for upper-class Fergus Urvill is clearly established, along with an additional personal motive for a later revenge.

The next strand in the past narrative concerns Kenneth, his return home to Lochgair from Glasgow University, and the circumstances of his meeting with Mary Lewis, whom he later marries. Their children, of course, include Prentice. Kenneth becomes an English teacher in the local high school, and continues living in Lochgair. His younger sister Fiona marries Fergus Urvill, who uses his inherited wealth to buy the ruined Gaineamh Castle with the object of restoring it as his family dwelling. Over a period of time Kenneth notices that his sister's marriage to Fergus seems to be under some strain. Yet there is a seemingly accidental tragic outcome to this marriage when there is a serious car crash in which Fiona is killed and Fergus is badly injured.

Another element in the family saga concerns Kenneth's younger brother Rory who is seen initially in the role of observer, first of his brother's courting of Mary Lewis and later of Fergus's sexual advances towards Fiona at Kenneth's wedding. He becomes a bit of a drifter, embracing a hippy style of life in the 1960s and 1970s, living in a squat in London, travelling around India, and trying to make a living as a writer. He writes poems and a successful book about his travels, but later finds it difficult to follow up this with another work. Rory's notes for a writing project entitled "The Crow Road" come into Prentice's hands and provide important evidence. He revisits Lochgair and his family there from time to time and introduces them to his girlfriend Janice Rae and her daughter Marion. However, it is Rory's mysterious disappearance in 1981 that provides a major focus for the action of *The Crow Road*, and it is the events causing this disappearance that need to be resolved by the end.

There is a strong imaginative and creative side to Kenneth, which comes out mainly in the stories he makes up to entertain his children and their friends. These stories, often told to them in the open countryside above Lochgair and making a deep and lasting impression on some of them, become the inspiration for Kenneth's second career as a successful children's writer. His stories are published and make his name to the extent that Rory feels some jealousy for him. They also give Kenneth such a degree of financial security that, when he is accidentally killed in the course of the novel, Prentice is astonished to find that he, along with the rest of the family, becomes moderately prosperous and financially independent by the terms of his father's will.

(c) 1979-1980: Rory's narrative

When Prentice visits Janice Rae, his 'Aunty Janice', at her flat in Crow Road in Glasgow, he is given a folder marked 'CR' containing Rory's notes and fragmentary writings on his intended new book. He feels that this folder will contain clues to Rory's disappearance, but his investigation is frustrated by his carelessness in leaving the folder on a train in Glasgow. However, the real evidence is found by Prentice and Ashley Watt on old computer disks left in Lochgair by Rory years before and found by Prentice in his father's desk as he sorts through Kenneth's papers. Once the files stored on these disks are opened, they reveal writings in a fictional style done by Rory which point to the truth about his sister Fiona's death and suggest a possible reason for Rory's disappearance.

These writings are presented in three sections at intervals within the narrative of *The Crow Road* and can be identified visually by being in italics.

The first section (pp.201-211), written in the third person from Rory's point of view, describes how he and Fergus Urvill become friendly when Rory is back at Lochgair trying to work out what direction his life should take. It is an unlikely friendship between an ex-hippy left-wing drifter and unsuccessful writer on the one hand and an arch-conservative landowner and capitalist factory owner on the other. Yet they are brothers-in-law through Fiona's marriage to Fergus, and it is this that they talk about one night in an old shooting lodge after a day's fishing and shooting. Fergus's tongue has been loosened by whisky and the unaccustomed effects of sharing a cannabis joint with Rory. He is clearly deeply unhappy by events in his marriage and he needs to talk in confidence to someone. What he tells Rory is not yet revealed, but it has the effect of putting an end to their closeness. Shortly afterwards Rory returns to London.

The second section (pp.245-253) deals with what Fergus told Rory about his wife Fiona, filled out with circumstantial detail by Rory as he reconstructs the events. At a family party given by Kenneth's older brother Hamish, and described also from Kenneth's point of view (pp.240-245), Fergus gets very drunk and passes out. His wife Fiona decides to drive him home and Lachy Watt, who is at the party, offers to give her a hand with Fergus when she gets him back to Gaineamh Castle, which has just been restored. They put Fergus to bed in a guest room and then leave him asleep as they go off to have a drink together. Later Fergus wakes up and tries to find his way back to his own bedroom. However, he finds to his surprise that he is locked out of that section of the castle. Thinking that he is being punished for getting drunk and feeling more sober, he decides to show how clever he is. He knows a way through the roof space past the new observatory he has had built on top of the castle; this way will take him to his own bedroom which he can enter by a hatch in the ceiling. He makes his way with some difficulty through the dark spaces and over the roof joists until he reaches the hatch. When he slightly opens it, he has a view down into the bedroom and sees Fiona and Lachy Watt together in bed engaged in sex. Fergus says and does nothing, but makes his way back silently the way he has come.

The final section of Rory's narrative (pp.289-296) describes the final minutes of Fiona's life as she sits with Fergus in his Aston Martin DB6 driving home along the side of Loch Fyne very fast after a dinner party with friends. She and Fergus are quarrelling about how their hostess had seemed to Fiona to be making sexual advances to a drunken Fergus. Fiona reflects in a state of desperation about how empty her life with Fergus is. Fergus is no longer interested in her and they seem to be staying together 'for the sake of the children'. Her marriage, her whole life, seems to be a failure. Fiona considers her possibilities, to leave Fergus finally or to stay and try to muddle through. As she does so, she sees Fergus look over at her and smile. Just before the powerful car crashes at full speed into the trees on a corner, she sees tears in his eyes.

Rory wrote no more of his fictionalised account of his sister's death. After reading his uncle's narrative, Prentice deduces that Rory had finally put it all together in his head as he was writing the final section and had gone off on a borrowed motorbike to confront Fergus. Nobody ever saw him alive again. The knowledge that Rory had acquired from Fergus had become a dangerous secret which provided the reason for his disappearance.

(d) 1980-1989: Prentice's memories

Part of the story of *The Crow Road* is made up of Prentice McHoan's recollections of growing up in Lochgair and observing his family and friends over the years of his childhood and adolescence. Some of these memories are recent, as when he recollects his long conversation with his grandmother Margot as he pushes her in her wheelchair through the grounds of Lochgair six months before her fatal accident, a conversation in which they discuss the family and Margot says that she thinks that Uncle Rory has been dead for the last eight years. Some of the memories go over several years to Prentice's boyhood and involve his relationship with his father Kenneth. He remembers his father's stories both as told directly to him and as read in his father's books. The relationship was close in those early years, but as Prentice moves through adolescence, the usual change occurs and Prentice finds himself at odds with Kenneth. In a reversal of the more common father-son conflict in Scottish novels, where the sensitive liberal-minded son falls foul of his father's stern religious beliefs, Prentice feels that Kenneth's tolerant atheism and sceptical attitudes to life do not satisfy his need to believe in something, to find some meaning behind the tragedies of life. This comes to a head over the death in a road accident of Prentice's closest friend Darren Watt, an artist. Kenneth and his son fall out while discussing this pointless death, as well as other family losses like the death of Prentice's Aunt Fiona and the disappearance of Rory (whom Kenneth believes to be still alive travelling abroad somewhere). Prentice moves out of the family home and lives first with his Aunt Ilsa in London and then with his Uncle Hamish in Gallanach.

Some of Prentice's memories concern his Uncle Rory before his disappearance. Being the youngest of his uncles, Rory seems to have a rapport with Prentice and can communicate with him more sympathetically than other members of the family. So Rory's disappearance has a special quality of loss for Prentice, and when he comes to realise that there is some mystery attached to the disappearance, he is impelled to follow up the clues that keep coming into his possession. The folder given to him by Janice Rae, the information from Ashley that someone has been deceiving a member of the McHoan family for a long time, the matchbox covers that he discovers in his father's desk which have been sent anonymously to Kenneth over a period of years, the identification of the possible sender of these covers as a friend of Fergus Urvill: these clues give focus to Prentice's loss and impetus to his search for the truth. As he works at the mystery, memories return to him that take on an added significance in the light of his new knowledge; the visit to his Uncle Fergus in hospital during which Fergus stresses the point the he doesn't understand why his wife wasn't wearing her seatbelt; the sight of the television correspondent Rupert Paxton-Marr shooting a protected bird, a buzzard, on Fergus's land; a conversation with Uncle Rory about a secret that someone had told him and which he had thought was a dream.

There are aspects of Prentice's past life that are not part of the memories relevant to the novel. For instance, there is hardly any reference at all to his school life before he goes to Glasgow University. The exclusion of this important element in his life has the effect of making the family focus of the action even more concentrated. The only game that we hear of him playing as a child is with his brother Lewis, when they adapt a non-violent board game devised by Kenneth to their own preferences, creating a war game that satisfies their appetite for violence, so disapproved of by their liberal pacifist-minded father. Even Prentice's developing sexual urges are kept within the extended family, as when he conducts a sexual experiment with Marion Rae, his Uncle Rory's girlfriend's daughter, on the back seat of his grandmother's garaged Lagonda car, with disastrous results to the car. (Later, as we see in the primary narrative, when he is in his final university year, he has a night of passionate sex with Marion's mother, Janice Rae, when they meet again after several years.) The first serious crush he develops is on his cousin Verity Walker, Uncle Fergus's niece, an infatuation which leads to a massive disappointment when his brother Lewis beats him once more in the sexual contest and marries her. The irony is that the true love of his life has been there all the time in the shape of Ashley Watt, whose nose he had once broken when they were at school.

So the fragmentary memories related by Prentice in the course of his progress towards a resolution of the mystery of Uncle Rory and his own personal difficulties with growing up have a necessary selective quality about them. They do not add up to a

'Life of Prentice McHoan', but are the necessary background to the specific concerns of the main action, the events of the 'present time', the primary narrative of the novel structure.

(e) November 1989 to March 1991: Prentice's main narrative
The primary narrative, or foreground events, of the novel concerns Prentice's own actions and feelings over a period of nearly a year and a half starting with the day of his grandmother's funeral. When the novel begins, he is a final year student at Glasgow University, trying to complete his honours degree at a time when he is experiencing a major personal problem; he is estranged from his father and is refusing to live at home or to accept any financial support from his family. During the months that follow, other concerns press upon him. He is seriously disappointed in love, he suffers a major bereavement, and he feels a growing obligation to find out the reason for the disappearance of his Uncle Rory eight years before. The resolution of these matters forms the main thread of the story. By following the events chronologically through the successive months, we shall be able to see the main development of the novel on which all the other narratives depend.

1989. November
At the funeral of Margot with its farcical conclusion, we see the main members of the McHoan family, plus some Urvills and Watts. It emerges that Prentice is estranged from his father Kenneth and staying with his Uncle Hamish, that he is infatuated with his cousin Verity Walker, and has an easy companionable relationship with his other female cousin Ashley Watt. After the funeral reception at Uncle Fergus's home in Gaineamh Castle, Prentice meets Ashley at the pub in Gallanach and later as he walks with her to her home, Ashley tells him about a meeting she had in Berlin with a man who told her that someone living locally called McHoan was the object of a deception over a long period of time. She hadn't found out any more. This is the beginning of the unravelling of the Uncle Rory mystery.

December
Back at university in Glasgow, Prentice is with his flatmate Gavin in a pub in Byres Road listening to his older brother Lewis as he does his stand-up comedy act. Lewis has been making a reputation for himself as a performer and missed his grandmother's funeral because he was in Australia. Suddenly Prentice

is greeted by a woman who turns out to be his Uncle Rory's girl-friend Janice Rae. They go back to her flat in Crow Road, and in the course of the evening, before they go to bed together and make passionate love, she gives Prentice a folder marked "C.R." that contains Uncle Rory's notes for a book he had been planning. Janice also tells Prentice about the last day that she had seen Rory, the day of his disappearance. When Prentice goes through the folder, he finds a clue suggesting there is another folder somewhere which may have information about a secret connected with Gallanach. At the end of the month Prentice goes back home for Christmas and New Year, driven by Verity Walker, with whom Lewis seems very friendly.

1990. January
There is a New Year party at Gaineamh Castle at which Prentice enjoys himself fully until he happens to see his brother Lewis and Verity Walker together embracing intimately. In a mood of self-pity he leaves the party and walks away alone. Next day at a family party at Uncle Hamish's house where he sees Lewis and Verity being very close and loving, Prentice disgraces himself completely. He gets very drunk and becomes loud-mouthed and insulting, especially about Lewis and Verity, so that the party is ruined and he has to be put to bed. Next day Prentice remembers little until his mother fills him in about his behaviour. He makes apologies to some of the people he has offended, but does nothing to heal the rift with his father and returns to Glasgow by train. He is feeling so bad that he forgets his bag and leaves it on the train. It contains not only the folder from Janice but another given to him by his mother, which contained a lot more of Rory's writings. Although he tries hard with the railway Lost Property, the bag does not turn up and he thinks it is lost for ever.

February – March
Back again at university, Prentice is feeling very low. Janice Rae has taken up with his flatmate Gavin, so that Prentice feels sexually slighted even more. Janice tells a little more about the possible secret known by Uncle Rory; it involved something serious that had been seen, perhaps by Rory himself. Prentice's studies begin to suffer as he loses interest in his work. Oppressed by the conflict with his father Kenneth, he refuses to use any money from home and is reduced to a life of poverty.

April – May
The deterioration in Prentice's life and attitudes continues. He
has given up trying to get his bag back from the railway. His
depression is intensified by the news from his mother that Lewis
and Verity are going to get married.

June
By midsummer, Prentice has been reduced to trying to steal a
book from a shop to sell for money. He has been charged with
shoplifting and is due to appear in court. Ashley takes him out for
a meal and takes him to task about the state he has allowed
himself to fall into. Prentice knows he has failed his university
finals and does not intend going back for resits the following year.
Ashley is interested in talking all this through with Prentice to
straighten him out, but when they return to Prentice's flat, Gavin
and Janice tell them that news has come of the death of Kenneth
McHoan. Ashley tries to comfort Prentice and drives him home to
Lochgair. Uncle Hamish tells Prentice about the circumstances of
Kenneth's death, how he was struck by lightning and fell off a
church steeple which he was climbing while drunk. Prentice sits
alone by the sea remembering his father and all the good things
about him, his stories and his concern that his children should
inherit his rationalism and humanist principles; so Prentice
comes closer to an understanding of his father and a resolution of
their disagreement over faith and religion. Lewis and Prentice
share the task of digging their father's grave in the garden of the
Lochgair house, and Lewis reveals that Verity is pregnant.
Prentice agrees to be his brother's best man.

July
Curiously, despite his father's death, Prentice is coming out of his
depression and apathy. Now reconciled to the marriage of Lewis
and Verity and with a sense of being in harmony with his family
again, Prentice learns that he has indeed failed his university
finals. However, the terms of Kenneth's will have made Prentice
(and the rest of his family) relatively prosperous and he decides to
return to university for another year to make up for his failure.
While going through his father's papers in his desk, Prentice
discovers another folder with more of Rory's notes and writings,
and, most significantly, an envelope with some computer disks
which will probably reveal more evidence when the files are
opened up. As he returns to Glasgow after all the business
surrounding his father's death has been concluded, Prentice has a

kind of vision. A field that he had observed from the train in
January in the midst of depression and seen as coarse and dismal
is now black because the grass has been burnt off, except where
the well-trodden grass has been left untouched in a bright green
cross. Looking at it, Prentice utters the last word spoken by his
dying father to Hamish, "See?"

October
The action jumps to the wedding of Lewis and Verity. As best man,
Prentice is in Highland dress, and is very involved in the bustle of
the reception held at home. He gives Ashley the envelope with
Rory's out-dated computer disks, so that she can use her computer
expertise and contacts to get them opened up. In return, Ashley
says that she has something to show Prentice and goes back to her
home to get it. While he waits, Prentice stands looking at his
father's grave with its new black stone memorial. When she
returns, Ashley shows Prentice a video of a television correspondent, Rupert Paxton-Marr, who was the man whom she had
met in Berlin who told her about the deception of the McHoans.
For his part, Prentice shows her the matchbox covers that he had
discovered in his father's desk, items that had been sent to his
father anonymously from different parts of the world over several
years and which Kenneth had believed came from Rory, proving
that he was still alive somewhere. The wedding reception
continues and Prentice throws himself into it, drinking a lot, and
smoking some joints and snorting coke with his friends. In the
wider international context, the Gulf crisis is brewing up.

November
By this month, Prentice has sorted himself out. He has been
cleared of the shoplifting charge, with the aid of an expensive
lawyer; he has returned to university and is living on his own in a
fine luxurious rented flat; and he has done some investigating of
the events surrounding Rory's disappearance by talking to the
police and to Rory's old flatmate who had lent him his motorbike
on that last day, but without turning up anything significant. So
finally Prentice flies to London to meet Ashley and confront
Paxton-Marr with the evidence that he has been helping to deceive
the McHoan family about Rory's disappearance. However, Paxton-
Marr refuses to speak to him and Prentice is left frustrated.
Nevertheless, he has remembered the occasion when, as a boy, he
had seen Paxton-Marr shooting on Fergus's land. So there is some
substance to his possible involvement in the Rory business.

December

At the end of the month, on the last day of the year, Prentice is back in Lochgair. An envelope has arrived for him containing the print-out of the contents of Rory's computer files, opened up by one of Ashley's contacts in the USA. However, Prentice delays opening the envelope. He goes around sightseeing with Lewis and Verity in the morning and in the afternoon as they stand on the battlements of the Castle, he eventually opens the envelope and begins to read the narratives created by Rory out of the family secret he had been told, the events leading up to Fiona's death. By the time he has finished, Prentice is aware of the truth about this death and has realised the reason for Rory's disappearance, especially as Verity is talking innocently about the layout under the castle roof and the hatch in the ceiling of Fergus's bedroom. With a kind of horror, he looks up at the sky with the others where his Uncle Fergus is flying past in his new Cessna aircraft. Later in the day as he drives to Glasgow Airport to meet Ashley, Prentice puts the last piece of the jigsaw together, how Fergus had murdered his wife in revenge for her betrayal of him by releasing her seatbelt just before driving deliberately off the road. He convinces Ashley of the truth of this by means of a painful demonstration.

1991. January

Prentice and his friends and family see in the New Year in a cheerful frame of mind, unlike the previous New Year. The only damper to Prentice's mood is that Ashley does not turn up, having gone off with somebody else at a party. Prentice realises that he has been too slow and comes to an awareness of his true feelings for Ashley, that he loves her. However, it seems that he is too late, since she returns south without their having another chance to meet. When Prentice himself returns to Glasgow, he decides to press the business of Uncle Rory's disappearance to a conclusion. He obtains Lachlan Watt's telephone number in Australia and eventually, as the Gulf War breaks out in air raids and devastation, he summons up his resolve and phones Australia. He asks directly whether Lachy had ever slept with his Aunt Fiona; Lachlan's response is to put the phone down without speaking. Prentice is left uncertain about what this means. His next step is to return to Lochgair, where he is appalled to learn that his mother has accepted an invitation from Fergus to go to the opera in Glasgow. He writes down his suspicions about Fergus on a piece of paper which he leaves in his father's desk, and goes to

Gaineamh Castle to confront his uncle with the matter. Fergus coolly denies everything and very reasonably suggests that Prentice is not thinking clearly under the strain of his father's death. However, Prentice is convinced of Fergus's guilt. That night an intruder breaks into the Lochgair house, apparently intent on obtaining the computer disks and starting a fire. Prentice fights with him and drives him off; even though the intruder is masked, Prentice recognises that it is Fergus. The police arrive but Prentice does not reveal that he knows who the intruder was. After a day or two Prentice returns to Glasgow and things seem to return to normal.

A sudden sequence of events, however, brings everything to a head and a rapid conclusion. Prentice learns later from Fergus's housekeeper that an international phone call has been received by Fergus; he deduces that it was Lachlan following up on Prentice's call. The following morning Fergus leaves his house and drives to the airstrip where he keeps his Cessna. Before he takes off he makes a phone call. Then he flies off out over the Atlantic until his plane runs out of fuel and crashes into the sea. Fergus's body is not recovered. The phone call he made was to the Strathclyde Police, giving an anonymous tip-off about drugs being hidden in a loch near Gallanach; when the loch is dragged, a body is recovered tied to a motorbike. The body is identified as that of Rory McHoan, and there are signs that he had been murdered by blows to the head from a smooth round object. The mystery of Uncle Rory's disappearance has been solved.

February
Once the police have released Rory's body to his family, it is laid to rest beside that of his brother Kenneth in the garden of the McHoan house.

March
This month sees the final resolution of the novel's action. On the 2nd Verity gives birth to a son. On the 8th Prentice goes to the reading of Fergus's will and finds that his uncle has left him his Bentley car with its contents. Inside it he finds a box containing a glass paperweight, which Prentice realises is the weapon that was used to kill his Uncle Rory. At Fergus's memorial service a week later, Prentice is filled with anger and finally loses any sense of a need for faith or religious belief, a feeling that he works out more clearly in his mind a few days later as he stands on a headland at the Butt of Lewis, the nearest place he can get to the spot in the

ocean where Fergus died. He throws the paperweight out into the sea. Back in Glasgow he meets Ashley, who has lost her job in London and is about to go to Canada. After a meal, they go back to Prentice's flat and make love. The following morning, Prentice is devastated to realise that Ashley is still intending to go away to Canada. However, she promises to return in June and they part, fully committed to each other and aware that their future will be shared. Back in Lochgair again, Prentice's mother is glad to hear that he is going to sell the Bentley and reveals that she knows more about him than he had thought. The novel ends with Prentice, Lewis, Verity and Diana Urvill on the battlements of Gaineamh Castle sharing a bottle of malt whisky and using a drop of it to christen the new generation of the family with the name of his grandfather, Kenneth McHoan.

Themes in the novel

Family and roots
As we have seen, Iain Banks has described *The Crow Road* as a family saga. The word 'saga' implies a story on a large scale, perhaps treated in a traditional way. A famous model or parallel might be *The Forsyte Saga* by John Galsworthy, a sequence of novels in which the story of a prosperous middle-class family is traced from the mid-nineteenth century down to the years after the First World War in the twentieth century. As a family, the Forsytes exist in both space and time. They are associated with a particular part of the country and their fortunes are traced through several generations. As time passes, the members of different branches of the family grow apart from each other, although there is a slight counter-movement back together when individuals meet and marry. The same tendencies can be observed on a smaller scale in *The Crow Road*. The McHoan family have their roots in a particular area of Argyll, and the family home passes down through more than one generation. They make their connections with other families, and as an extended family, or 'clan', with several branches, extra links of love and marriage are made within the total related group.

There seems to be a two-way movement operating within the narrative of *The Crow Road*. One direction of movement is outward from the family's central location between Crinan and Loch Fyne, a physical departure or a psychological detachment from home. The other movement is inward in terms of personal relationships between some characters who tend to seek their enduring personal relationships and find their lives' fulfilment within the context of the family.

The outward movement can be seen principally in the way in which many of the characters seem to move out from the traditional heartland to seek new spheres of action or experience. Thus, in Kenneth McHoan's generation, his sister Ilsa moves away and makes her life elsewhere, becoming a regular traveller to distant parts of the world. Rory cannot settle at home and travels abroad, making his reputation by writing about his travels in India. He continues to be restless and unsettled, living a kind of hippy existence and trying to make it as a writer. Kenneth himself, after seeming to settle down to be a teacher in a local school, breaks out of the routine and finds fame and prosperity as a writer of imaginative children's stories. In other branches of the 'family', Lachlan Watt escapes from his restricted working-class environment by first going to sea and later settling in Australia, and Fergus Urvill, although seemingly rooted in the comfortable life-style of the country gentleman and factory owner, has interests in history, archaeology and astronomy, leading him to restore the ruined Gaineamh Castle and build an observatory on top of it; he also has a restless adventurous streak that finds an outlet in fast sports cars and flying. In the next generation, Prentice's elder brother Lewis is carving out a successful career for himself as a stand-up comedian. Diana and Helen, the twin daughters of Fergus and Fiona Urvill, find very different niches in life, Helen as a banker in Switzerland and Diana, inspired all unknowingly by Prentice, as an astronomer in Hawaii. Before his life was tragically cut short, Darren Watt was beginning to arouse controversy as an abstract artist and sculptor, whereas his sister Ashley is a computer expert finding work in different parts of the world. Thus, from their home base in traditional Scotland, the McHoan family and its related branches are reaching out into the wider world with its infinite variety and opportunities. Prentice, already in his twenties, seems to be an exception in that he has no articulate aspirations to move away from the world he has grown up in. Although he studies in Glasgow and is estranged from his father, he is always ready to return to the family fold. As his name is intended to suggest, he is still an apprentice in life and needs to come to a condition of self-knowledge before his path opens clearly before him.

The inward movement of the narrative is visible in the contained quality of the emotional and sexual relationships dealt with in the novel. After the links between the McHoans and the

Urvills and Watts are established, there is a tendency for further entanglements to be worked out within the family circle. The adultery of Fiona with Lachlan Watt, and the potential interest of Fergus in Prentice's mother, the widow of his brother-in-law Kenneth, demonstrate this in the elder generation, while the younger generation are similarly inward-looking. The rivalry of Prentice and Lewis in relation to their cousin Verity; Prentice's sexual interludes with his Uncle Rory's former girl-friend Janice Rae, and earlier with her daughter Marion; and finally his realisation that his true love is his other remoter cousin Ashley Watt: these contain the emotional scope of the novel within the boundaries of a defined circle of linked individuals.

Yet there is a larger context within which the action of the novel operates, preventing it from seeming to be a purely local or parochial set of events. As the main narrative of *The Crow Road* moves to its climax of revelation, events on the world stage are similarly moving towards a point of violent explosion. The developing political and military crisis in the Gulf in 1990 becomes noticeable through the eyes of Prentice as a backdrop to the gradual resolution of the Uncle Rory mystery, and the final solution for Prentice is accompanied by the outbreak of the Gulf War itself in early 1991 with the bombing of Iraq by the United Nations.

The quest for truth

On the surface, *The Crow Road* is a novel where the main action is the progress towards the solution of a mystery, the disappearance of Rory McHoan. So in some respects it has parallels with the genre of the detective story. There is a matter needing investigation, which turns out to be a crime; indeed there are two crimes revealed by the end. There is a possible victim (in fact, ultimately two). There is a 'villain', a murderer whose guilt is finally established. And there is a 'private detective' figure, whose efforts put him in some danger but are eventually successful. The classic stories in the genre are those about Sherlock Holmes by Arthur Conan Doyle or, later, those by Raymond Chandler about the American private eye, Philip Marlowe. In the more modern characterising of the detective, he or she is flawed and inconsistent, often undergoing great personal trauma in the investigation and becoming deeply involved with the mystery. In discovering the truth, the detective comes to a state of greater self-knowledge. There are clues to the truth, which have to be studied and correctly interpreted, and frequently, unlike the ideal

Holmes figure, the detective misunderstands them and becomes confused. Such a story is a modern equivalent of the allegorical romance, a traditional story in which a hero or heroine seeks a great prize and experiences many adventures and setbacks in the face of danger before the prize is obtained. It is often a quest for Truth, which may have a religious significance. The Truth in traditional story produces a transformation in the hero figure and may bring salvation.

In *The Crow Road* the quest seems to operate on more than one level. There is the main quest in realistic terms, the search by Prentice, with the help of the faithful Ashley, for the truth about his Uncle Rory's disappearance. There is an unconscious search by Prentice for love and fulfilment in his apparently aimless life. And there is a linked search by Prentice for the truth about faith and religious belief, a truth that will satisfy him and be his own rather than what his father and others try to give him. All this questing goes on at the same time and comes to a resolution at almost the same moment. By the end of the novel, Prentice has gained the prize (or prizes) and his life is to an extent transformed. He has solved the mystery of Rory; he has realised the true object of his love, a love that is returned; and he has come to a personal philosophical standpoint, a sense that all the gods are false, echoing his father's scepticism.

The quest for the truth about his uncle's disappearance does not proceed steadily. After the initial impetus given to Prentice's investigation by the acquisition of two of Rory's folders, one from Janice Rae and the other from his mother, there is a serious setback when he loses them on the Glasgow train. There follows a period of stagnation and depression when Prentice is oppressed by his own problems and has no luck in his efforts to trace the lost bag with the folders and Darren's scarf. The bag never turns up, but when fresh clues are discovered among Prentice's father's papers, the investigation takes off again and moves steadily towards the uncovering of Fergus Urvill as the person responsible for two deaths.

Similarly, Prentice's love life has its frustrations. The early experimentation on the back seat of his grandmother's Lagonda car with Marion Rae resulted in a disastrous collapse of the vehicle and led to the discovery that even then his brother Lewis was to be reckoned with as a dangerous rival. This is confirmed when, after Prentice's gaining of valuable experience with an older woman, Janice Rae, he finds that Lewis has acted more positively with Verity Walker, the object of Prentice's infatuation.

The result of this is that Prentice has to watch in frustration as Lewis and Verity's relationship develops into an engagement and subsequent marriage, with an accompanying pregnancy and the birth of their son Kenneth, Prentice's nephew. All this while, the girl he is really in love with, though he has not yet realised this, is in his life regularly, one of his circle of friends socially, concerned about his difficulties, ready to help and comfort him, and an associate in his search for the truth about Rory. Ashley Watt is created by Banks as a strong-minded, intelligent, independent, attractive young woman, the kind of novel heroine that Banks uses again and again in both his mainstream novels and his science fiction. The love which Prentice feels for her and which is returned by her is the major truth that Prentice has to discover.

Prentice McHoan's quest for something to believe in is a major philosophical strand in the novel. From what is found in other novels and writings by Iain Banks, it is clear that Banks' attitude to organised traditional religion is one of scepticism, even hostility. In the later novel, *Whit,* to be dealt with in the next section, religion is perhaps the main theme of the story. Here, in *The Crow Road*, Banks makes religion a continuing theme that colours some of the feelings and problems experienced by his main character. Prentice observes two of his close relations, his father Kenneth and his Uncle Hamish, at close hand. In his father he sees a convinced scepticism about all religion and faith; Kenneth is a convinced atheist, liberal and tolerant in his views, but prepared to try to persuade his family by means of his imaginative stories and evocations of natual history to reject religious explanations of the universe. Uncle Hamish, on the other hand, has created a religion of his own, a cruel creed of immediate punishment in the after-life for all evil done or inspired by a person in this world, in which God is seen as a kind of celestial accountant transferring pain and suffering from one soul to another as a massive exercise in balancing the books. It is a parody of the traditional beliefs in hell and damnation, a personal sadistic fantasy which Prentice calls a "unique brand of condemnationist Christianity" (p.176).

As far as it goes, this is a straightforward setting of two alternative views against each other. There is no in-between point of moderate religious belief or compassionate faith. It might be expected that the scales are loaded by Banks in favour of Kenneth McHoan's imaginative materialism. This is certainly so. Uncle Hamish's beliefs are seen to be ridiculous, rightly shunned and ignored even by his wife and children. Kenneth's lack of belief is supported by good humour and reason and creative fantasy. Yet

Banks makes the issue more complicated by combining the religious element with a common feature of novels dealing with different family generations, the idea of a father-son conflict. As was pointed out in the treatment of *The Wasp Factory*, the father-son opposition in several Scottish literary texts has been based partly on a disagreement over religious matters, the father representing an older generation's belief in a stern Calvinist morality, the son expressing the more liberal views of a new Enlightenment generation. There is a historical location for this in the Scotland of the late eighteenth down to the early twentieth century. In *The Wasp Factory*, Banks created a father-'son' scenario in which the father represented and acted out the part of a man driven by Science rather than Religion. Here, in *The Crow Road*, Banks turns the whole situation around; it is the father who is the Enlightenment figure, inspired by liberal-minded passion and scientific materialism, and the son, Prentice, who is the supporter of faith and religious belief, although as yet he has not found the nature of such a belief. Prentice's rebellion against his father takes him no further than a physical and emotional estrangement; he does not actively look for a religious truth, and so perhaps it is not really a quest. Yet he does move from troubled doubt to a state of certainty by the end of the novel.

Initially Prentice is moved by the sudden apparently pointless death of his friend Darren in a road accident, and by a memory of the death of his Aunt Fiona in a similar happening some years before, to discuss with his father his feeling that there has to be more than just this life, something that continues after death, to set against the pointlessness and cruelty of the things that happen to humanity. His father rejects this notion as irrational in the face of human insignificance within the massive indifferent universe, arguing that there is no momentum, no continuity, in human life. Prentice angrily accuses his father of being overbearing in his negative arguments, and the separation between them begins. It is only after Kenneth's death that Prentice begins to look at the matter more calmly; remembering all the family deaths, his father's wonderful stories, and his father's unselfish anxiety that his children should be prepared for life, an anxiety that could sometimes become an oppressive tendency to attempt their brainwashing. It is the final set of events in the novel that brings Prentice to his state of certainty. The anger he feels against Fergus for the death of Rory causes him to reject any search for something to believe in; "All the gods are false" is the thought that Prentice holds to at Fergus's memorial service as he looks up at the tower that killed his father. When he stands on the clifftop in Lewis, after throwing the paperweight out to sea, his thoughts become clarified. Life had no momentum, no continuity, and "the world is neither fair nor unfair...... the old man had been right and I had been wrong." (p.485) "The belief that we somehow moved on to something else – whether still recognisably ourselves, or quite thoroughly changed – might be a tribute to our evolutionary tenacity and our animal thirst for life, but not to our wisdom. That saw a value beyond itself; in intelligence, knowledge and wit as concepts – wherever and by whoever expressed – not just in its own personal manifestation of those qualities, and so could contemplate its own annihilation with equanimity, and suffer it with grace; it was only a sort of sad selfishness that demanded the continuation of the individual spirit in the vanity and frivolity of a heaven." (pp.484-485)

Prentice is not the only character who changes his views about religion. Broken by the death of his younger brother, Uncle Hamish rejects his previous personal religion as a delusion and returns to the traditional belief in God as a stern father who will punish his children out of love.

The Crow Road is therefore a novel in which the ideas of religion are both seriously and light-heartedly explored. The whole action of the novel is framed by two occasions of traditional religious significance; the funeral of the last of the older generation, Margot, and the christening of the first of the new generation. However, the former occasion literally explodes in a farcical climax and the latter is a secular ceremony in which young Kenneth McHoan is baptised with whisky on the castle battlements. The death of the atheist Kenneth McHoan is presented as an event that some traditional believers would see as a Divine punishment; he is struck by lightning as he drunkenly climbs up the outside of the local church steeple and falls to his death, striking his head on a gravestone. Yet it is no more than a meaningless accident. Similarly Prentice has a vision of a luminous green cross in a field seen from the train; it too has no significance, being only the chance result of the burning-off of the grass. In both cases, the reaction of the persons involved is the one word, "See!" The suggestion of the word is that something has been proved, but Banks leaves it to the reader to deduce what it might be. The ultimate note of the novel, felt by Prentice as he looks out from the castle, is an optimistic affirmation of life's most valuable forms, in the new-born child, in shared love and in the natural world.

Section Four

WHIT (1995)

Introduction

Just before the publication of *Whit*, Iain Banks gave an interview to *The Scottish Book Collector*, in which he discussed the progress of his work up to that date. Asked about his new novel, he said in his usual unserious manner, " It was going to be called *Whit*, then it was going to be called *Twenty-nine*..... we might even be a bit cheeky and try to get away with calling it *Cult Novel*." Eventually, of course, it was the first of these possible titles that was chosen. There are good reasons why this is a very suitable title, but the two discarded suggestions would both have had grounds for support.

Whit is a novel about a religious community, too loose and tolerant really to be branded as a cult in the present-day critical or hostile use of the word, in the years from its foundation in 1948 down to 1995, the present time of the action. The word 'cult' suggests a religious group of a very exclusive nature, too small and apart from mainstream social life to be regarded as a church. The Luskentyrian Sect of the Select of God have grown from a tiny beginning in Harris in the Outer Isles and now live and work on a small estate with a mansion house and farm beside the River Forth a few miles from Stirling. They have a few contacts, mainly past members of the community, in the world outside among the Unsaved, but generally live a very self-contained simple existence under the guidance of their founder and patriarch Salvador Whit. To the outside world they appear strange because of their beliefs and seemingly eccentric practices. In the eyes of the media, they are a love-cult, because one of their main religious observances is a quadrennial Festival of Love in May of the year before a leap year. This involves a lot of merrymaking and free lovemaking, the intention of which is to try to arrange the birth of Leapyearian children on or around the 29th of February. Such children would be of high status. Isis Whit, the granddaughter of Salvador, is such a Leapyearian and occupies a special place in the Community. The novel focuses on her as the main character, and follows her adventures between the 1st and the 14th May, 1995, a period in which there is a major change in her situation and outlook as a result of what happens to and around her.

Title of the novel

The significance of the title, therefore, is clear. 'Whit' is a name, referring both to an individual person, the eponymous heroine of the novel, Isis Whit, and to the family to which she belongs, stemming from the founder of the Community, Salvador Whit. Associations with 'Whit?', the Scots form of 'What?', and with the word 'whit', a small particle, as in the phrase, 'not a whit', are irrelevant distractions. But of course, 'Whit' means 'white' in a specific religious context. Whitsun is a Christian occasion, the seventh Sunday after Easter. The reference in the name is to the white robes worn by Christian converts in the early Church. Salvador Whit wears white robes as the head of the Luskentyrian Community. (Incidentally, another name for Whitsun is Pentecost, which was the occasion when the Holy Ghost descended upon the apostles of Christ and they spoke in tongues, or languages, other than their own. Part of the Luskentyrian ritual was to 'sing in tongues'; Isis says (p. 47) that "it sounds like nonsense, like babble, and yet through this glorious chaos we communicate.") There is an obvious set of cultural associations with 'white' – innocence, virginity, purity, the sacrificial lamb – and Isis is the embodiment of these in the novel. Her going forth into the World of the Unsaved puts all these to the test, and part of the resolution of the novel is how Isis, like Prentice McHoan in *The Crow Road*, comes to terms with her own self, her own situation, and achieves self-knowledge. Lurking behind 'Whit', or 'White', however, is its opposite, 'Black'. Black and White represent a traditional dualism, a coexistence of opposites, which was part of the Manichean belief, condemned as a heresy by the Church, that everything springs from the two equal opposing principles of good and evil, light and dark. This dualism is basic to the construction of the novel from the start. We can see it in a number of paired contrasts: Isis and her brother, Allan; the Saved of the Luskentyrian Sect and the Unsaved of the outside world; and the final revelation of the dual nature of Salvador Whit, who is both the White Saviour explicit in his adopted name and the former Army deserter and thief, Moray Black, cast up on the sands of Luskentyre in a reincarnation from the sea. ('Moray' is not only a Scottish name but a sea predator, a large carnivorous eel inhabiting the dark depths.)

Structure and narrative of the novel

As with *The Wasp Factory* and *The Crow Road*, *Whit* has a
chronological structure based on a set period of time during which
the main action is worked out. In *The Wasp Factory*, the
succession of days corresponded exactly with the sequence of
chapters. In *The Crow Road*, on the other hand, the complexities
of the different narratives bore no visible relation to the chapters
within which they were developed. There is a similar lack of
correspondence in *Whit* between the flow of narrative and the
division into chapters. However, it is of significance that the novel
is divided into twenty-nine chapters. Isis was born on the 29th
February, 1976, and was a Leapyearian; the number of chapters
clearly is a reference to the importance of this as an element
within the Luskentyrian set of beliefs.

Whit has a similar but much simpler narrative structure than
The Crow Road. The latter novel contained a number of different
character viewpoints and blended narratives from different times.
Whit contains only one character viewpoint, that of Isis, so that
the reader is always aware of the identity of the supposed
narrator. Yet within her narrative, there are distinct elements
similar to those that are found in *The Crow Road*. There is a
survey of the history of the Luskentyrian Sect from its founding in
September 1948 down to the present time of the novel; there is an
explanation of the religious beliefs of the Sect; there are Isis'
memories of her life in the Community prior to the main events;
and there is a primary narrative following the 'mission' of Isis to
the outside world from the 1st to the 14th May, 1995, and how she
finds the 'truth' about the Community and herself. A review of the
narrative of the novel can be done most conveniently by taking it
all in chronological order, and dealing with the religious and
philosophical ideas in a later section.

Synopsis of the novel

The origins of the Luskentyrian Sect go back to the stormy night of
the 30th September 1948 when two Asian sisters originally from
Khalmakistan, Aasni and Zhobelia Asis, are huddled in their
mobile shop van on a beach in Harris in the Outer Hebrides. They
have escaped from their family and the prospect of arranged
marriages, and are trying to make a living selling provisions round
the crofts. Now, as they shelter from the storm outside, they hear a
thump on the side of the van and, going outside, they discover a

young man, cold and wet and unconscious. From the word that he mutters, they decide that his name is Salvador, a name which he later decides was intended for him by God. Salvador feels that he has had a vision which points to a new life for him as a messenger of God and begins his career as the leader of a new religious movement. Aasni and Zhobelia join him as his 'wives' and co-founders of the Luskentyrian Sect which operates first on Harris and later, after 1954, at High Easter Offerance, an estate with a mansion house and a farm near Stirling donated to them by a convert, Mrs Woodbean. The Community grows slowly by means of interested visitors, occasional converts and the children born to Aasni and Zhobelia and other members of the group. Isis is the daughter of Christopher, also born on the 29th of February, the son of Salvador and Aasni. The Community progresses well until 1979, when a disastrous fire destroys half of the mansion house and kills Isis' parents and her grandmother Aasni. A year later, Zhobelia disappears from the Community, and her whereabouts are unknown. Isis grows up, goes to a neighbouring school, and is regarded as having a special status within the Community. Her elder brother Allan acts as the business and financial manager for the Community. As the novel opens, the Community is preparing itself for the forthcoming Festival of Love to be held at the end of May, an occasion in which Isis will be expected to participate for the first time. She has mixed feelings about this prospect.

Isis' memories do not go back as far as the 'Great Fire'. She has no memory of her parents, but her upbringing within the Community was one of security and shared parenting, with no sense of a lack of love. Her formal education at a nearby private school had passed without any real difficulties being caused by her connection with the Sect and its apparently strange practices. Some of her vivid memories are of her older cousin Morag, and of Sophi Woodbean, to whom she feels particularly close. Isis has never had a boyfriend; she is in many respects an innocent, although when she was assaulted by a man beside the river two years before, she had defended herself very effectively. The most significant incident of her childhood had occurred when she was quite small. Playing one day with her older brother Allan, she finds an apparently dead fox in a field. Allan is convinced it is quite dead, but Isis feels it can live again; holding it tight, she feels a force flowing out of her into the fox, which returns to life and runs off unharmed. In later years, Isis wonders what kind of power she has that can exercise action at a distance. It is only very late in the novel that she arrives at some understanding of this gift and its origin.

The main action, or primary narrative, of the novel covers Isis' experiences in the period from the 1st to the 14th May, 1995. It may be most appropriate to summarise these on a day by day basis.

Monday 1 May. The day begins with Isis going on foot to Dunblane to her organ practice in the Cathedral. After tea with the organist, she returns to High Easter Offerance to discover that a letter has come from her cousin Morag, a successful solo musician in London, to say that she will not be returning to the Community for the Festival of Love at the end of the month. After much discussion, it is decided that Isis will go on a mission to find Morag and persuade her to come back to the fold.

Tuesday 2 May. Isis sets off on her mission with the good wishes of the Community and an old kitbag containing her belongings and various items that she might need on her journey. She floats and paddles down the river Forth in a raft made out of the inner tube of a large motor tyre until she arrives on the outskirts of Edinburgh. She walks from there to the house of a friend and former member of the Community, Gertie Possil, who receives her as a blessed and honoured guest. The first stage of her journey is over.

Wednesday 3 May. Isis spends the day in Edinburgh trying to work out how she can continue her journey to London. The rules of the Luskentyrian Sect discourage her from paying to travel on modern transport in comfort and so she has to look for other means. Eventually she decides to stow away the following night on a freight train carrrying goods south. That morning she had discovered a treasure in her kitbag, a small glass jar containing 'zhlonjiz', the precious ointment of the Luskentyrian Sect, which she decides has been secretly given to her to help her on her mission.

Thursday 4 May. After another day in Edinburgh, Isis boards a freight train and hides in a new automobile being transported overnight to the London area.

Friday 5 May. Isis arrives in London in the morning and makes her way partly by bus (without paying) but mostly on foot to the house where her half-brother Zeb, or Zebediah, is squatting with some friends, including Boz and Declan. She spends the rest of the day with them, consuming a lot of cider before retiring rather drunk to her hammock in the attic.

Saturday 6 May. Isis and Zeb spend a fruitless day trying to track Morag down. She is no longer living at the address Isis has for her and her whereabouts are unknown; her agent is not to be

found at his Soho address; the London concert halls have no
knowledge of Morag as a soloist performing at concerts.
Discouraged and puzzled, Isis returns to Zeb's squat to ponder the
problem and attempt to commune with God seeking an answer.
She rubs on some of the *zhlonjiz* and swallows a little of it, but her
meditation produces no results; God does not communicate with
her. She rejoins the others and spends the evening with them
smoking cannabis joints before again retiring to her hammock
somewhat dizzily. As she lies there, Declan makes sexual
advances to her. When Isis tries to push him away, her hammock
collapses and they both fall through the floor of the loft into the
room below. Boz is there watching a pornographic video, and Isis
recognises the girl on the screen as her cousin Morag. Boz tells
her that it is in fact the celebrated porn star, Fusillada DeBauch.

Sunday 7 May. Isis views the porn video with mixed feelings
and confirms that the star is indeed Morag. Then she sets out
again with Zeb and Boz to track down Morag's agent in Soho.
They discover that he lives in a large house in an Essex village
and go there by train and taxi. However, at the house they are
driven off by a security guard and a large dog after it is discovered
that Morag is not in the house and apparently does not wish to
see Isis. All the same, by a clever ruse, Isis manages to obtain a
telephone number where Morag can be reached. On ringing the
number Isis finds out that it is a health farm in Somerset. They
return to London and on the way Isis deals successfully with an
aggressive group of young racist thugs.

Monday 8 May. Isis continues her search for Morag on her
own, hitch-hiking from London to the West Country. When she
has passed through Bath and Wells and is almost at her
destination, she is picked up by a group of New Age travellers on
their way to an open-air gathering near Glastonbury. She is
enjoying their company when they are suddenly stopped at a
roadblock by the police, who are preventing people of their hippy
type from proceeding further. Isis leaves the group when they
turn to go back and insists to the police that she has the right to
continue on her own way. As a result she is forcibly arrested, flung
into a police van and handcuffed; her kitbag is searched on
suspicion of containing drugs and her jar of *zhlonjiz* is smashed.
Isis is then taken to a police station where she has to spend the
night in a cell.

Tuesday 9 May. The following morning, Isis is rescued from
police custody by her American maternal grandmother, Yolanda
Cristofiori, accompanied by two lawyers. Yolanda had been

looking for Isis and seen her arrest on the local television news.
Yolanda takes Isis to her luxury hotel in Bath and Isis begins to
enjoy the alien pleasures of new clothes and expensive hotel
service. They go to the health farm but find that Morag has
checked out, having also seen on television that Isis was in the
neighbourhood. They then go back to the house in Essex but find
that it is dark and empty. Accordingly Yolanda takes Isis to the
Dorchester Hotel in London for the night and some more
materialistic luxury.

Wednesday 10 May. Isis and Yolanda fly from Heathrow to
Edinburgh and then drive in a hired car to High Easter Offerance.
On the way Isis becomes aware of Yolanda's suspicion of all
religions and cults, confirmed by the horrific events of Waco in
Texas, where a fanatical cult leader had caused the deaths of
many people, including children. Yolanda warns her granddaughter against the dangerous craziness and jealousy of men.
They arrive at High Easter Offerance, where Isis is astonished to
discover that she is in disgrace and under suspicion of betraying
the Luskentyrian Sect by stealing the precious *zhlonjiz*. On
thinking about what had happened, Isis comes to the conclusion
that she has been set up by somebody, who had planted the
zhlonjiz in her kitbag for her to find and use in the mistaken belief
that it was there by the wish of Salvador and the Community.
There was somebody in High Easter Offerance who was her
enemy. In the evening Isis is summoned to see her grandfather
Salvador and report what she had found out. However, it becomes
clear that he has a different purpose in mind when he begins to
make sexual advances to her and tries to seduce her forcibly. Isis
fights him off and leaves his presence in distress. She goes to her
friend Sophi Woodbean, who comforts her. They overhear a call on
the Woodbeans' telephone from Isis' Uncle Mohammed, who says
drunkenly that he will come for Isis the next day. Isis spends the
night in Sophi's bed.

Thursday 11 May. Isis discovers by chance that her brother
Allan has known all along where Morag was to be found. He is
clearly concealing this for his own purposes, which include
supplanting Isis as heir to Salvador and turning the Community
into a more capitalist and business-orientated enterprise. Uncle
Mohammed arrives in the Community and Isis tells him what has
been happening, although he does not seem very interested. Isis
agrees to go away with him the next day down to his home in the
North of England to get away from the Sect for a while. That
night, Isis breaks into her brother Allan's office and, hiding there,

overhears Allan talking on a forbidden mobile phone to Morag telling her lies about Isis acting in a crazy manner and having to be packed off with Uncle Mo. Left alone in the office, Isis also discovers that her Great-Aunt Zhobelia, who had disappeared years before, is alive and her whereabouts are known to Uncle Mo and others. When she gets back to Sophi's house, Isis telephones Morag directly at a number she found in Allan's papers and finds out from her that she had been receiving letters supposedly from Isis, expressing strong sexual obsession with Morag; Morag had been repelled by these and had tried to avoid contact with Isis. Similarly, someone had been sending letters to the Community supposedly from Morag. Realising that there is a serious deception being perpetrated, Isis arranges to meet Morag in Edinburgh the following day for a further discussion.

Friday 12 May. Isis sets off with Uncle Mo for the south by bus and train, after saying goodbye to a hostile Community. On the train she gets Uncle Mo drunk and worms the address of Great-Aunt Zhobelia out of him before leaving the train at Newcastle and making her way back to Edinburgh to meet Morag at the Royal Commonwealth Pool. Morag tells Isis how she had given up her music and got into porn movies. They discuss possible motives for Allan's treachery and agree to join forces to expose the plot at the special Full Moon Service of the Luskentyrian Sect at High Easter Offerance in two days time. Isis leaves Edinburgh for the town of Mauchtie, where Zhobelia is living in a private nursing home. She gets there in the evening, manages to enter Zhobelia's room secretly and introduces herself to her great-aunt. In the course of a long catching-up conversation, Isis learns many interesting things, such as the true nature of *zhlonjiz*, and obtains from Zhobelia evidence about Salvador's real identity, including an army passbook and an old ten-pound note, all that remains of the contents of the canvas bag that Salvador had with him when he was cast ashore on Harris nearly fifty years before. The great fire at High Easter Offerance had been caused by Aasni and Zhobelia burning the rest of the money, an accident that caused Zhobelia to leave the Community. The most significant thing that Isis learns, however, is that the gift of second sight, or having visions, that the Community had thought belonged to Salvador was in fact a power possessed by Zhobelia, a gift that seemed now to have been passed on to Isis as a power of healing. Zhobelia agrees to go back with Isis to the Community and try living there again.

Saturday 13 May. The following morning, Isis leaves Zhobelia and goes to Glasgow to do some research into Salvador's past. She stays with Topec, a cousin (but really her uncle). She discovers some interesting facts: that the ten-pound note had been part of a sum of money stolen from the army in 1948; that Salvador was in reality Moray Black, an army private who was wanted on suspicion of the theft; and that a ship called the 'Salvador' had been in a storm off the Hebrides a day after the theft and had lost some of its deck cargo. Isis has to face the unpleasant truth about the origins of the Luskentyrian Sect, and the true nature of its founder. After much thought in the night, she decides on what she has to do the following day.

Sunday 15 May. Isis telephones Sophi, who drives to Glasgow to pick her up. The two girls then go to Mauchtie and collect Zhobelia. They drive to Stirling and meet Morag at her hotel. Late in the afternoon, the four of them drive to High Easter Offerance, where Isis confronts Salvador and Allan and gives them an ultimatum. Isis is to become the effective leader of the Sect, which is to go on as before but with a little more democratic control; Salvador is to stay as the respected figurehead of the Community, but will be only a figurehead. Allan is to publicly confess his treachery towards Isis and the Community, but can continue as administrator under Isis' supervision. Otherwise, Isis will make sure that he is evicted from the Community. They are forced to agree, and the novel ends with Isis about to address the whole Community as its new leader enjoying the exercise of real power. It appears that her first action will be to tell the Truth about the past.

Themes in the novel

Family and community
Just like *The Wasp Factory* and *The Crow Road*, *Whit* is a novel centred on the relationships within a family. Yet, unlike the families of these novels, the family in *Whit* is a very extended family, involving sets of very complex and irregular relationships and including 'brothers' and 'sisters' with no direct blood links. The family is in fact a community that has grown up over three generations living and working together in an enclosed environment and governed by a set of distinctive rules. At its heart, the Luskentyrian Sect of the Select of God has the patriarch Salvador Whit, like a figure from the Old Testament of the Bible, part prophet, part clan chief. He is surrounded by his direct family consisting of his two 'wives' (now departed from the scene), his children by them and by other women, his

grandchildren and even great-grandchildren, and by his other
followers and disciples. Some of them have dispersed to other
parts of Britain and the world at large, but in time of need they
can be called upon to give support to the Sect and direct help to its
representatives, such as Isis.

Iain Banks is at pains to present a picture of the Luskentyrian
Community as being anything but repressive and unsympathetic.
The orphaned Isis and Allan are brought up in an atmosphere of
caring and supportiveness; the brothers and sisters of the
Community are employed usefully on tasks they undertake
voluntarily; no pressures are exerted on members of the
Community to stay on against their will; and donations to the
Sect are not demanded or enforced. It is this benevolent aspect of
the Sect that Isis sees as being under threat by Allan's secret
plans and which she aims to preserve by taking power herself at
the end. Quite apart from the religious doctrines that inspired it
and the questionable origins and motives of its founder, the
Luskentyre Community is a success in social and personal terms.

Male / female contrasts

Unlike the other two novels being dealt with in this guide, *Whit*
does not illustrate that common theme of the novel genre, the
father-son conflict. This is not merely because of the obvious facts
that Isis is a daughter and she has no living parents. There is
basically no conflict between one generation and the next in the
novel. Where we might expect to find such a conflict, between Isis
and her father figure, in fact her grandfather Salvador, there has
been a long-existing harmony, with Salvador favouring Isis over
her elder brother as his heir. This was not because of any gulf
between Salvador and Allan, but because of the special status of
Isis as a Leapyearian; what Allan feels is jealousy towards Isis,
not alienation from his grandfather. When Salvador acts violently
against Isis by striking her, it is because of his mistaken belief
that she has betrayed both him and the Community; and when he
gives way to his sexual desires in her presence, it is an aspect of
his chauvinist patriarchal attitudes towards all women, even his
blood relations.

The real sustained opposition within the novel is between male
and female qualities and characteristics. The traditional dualism
of light and dark, good and evil, is visible in ways already referred
to in an earlier section. However, Banks makes use of another
dualism, one that is a common element within the mystical
thought that derives from Buddhism, particularly Zen. That is the

concept of Yin and Yang, the complementary feminine and masculine principles. Traditionally, Yin is dark, passive and negative, the 'shadow', whereas Yang is bright, active and positive, the 'sun'; an opposition clearly devised by a male mind. Iain Banks very deliberately turns the concept completely around.

Throughout the novel, there is an explicit contrast between the male and the female characters. Gender difference carries with it a clear moral and psychological distinction, so the significant male characters illustrate one set of qualities, and female characters illustrate another opposing set. No living characters in the novel cross the basic divide.

The important male characters within the plot range from Salvador and Allan Whit at the heart of the Community to those outside the Community who are called upon in different ways to play their parts, such as Uncle Mohammed, and Zebediah and Topec. Without exception, these male characters are either seriously flawed or at least weak in their dealings with Isis and her quest. While both Zebediah in London and Topec in Glasgow are thoroughly amiable and help Isis in limited ways, they can be seen to have fallen away from the ideals and discipline of the Luskentyrians and are controlled more by their own pleasures and social habits than any concern for Isis' purposes. Uncle Mohammed, who is called in by Allan to take charge of Isis after her 'disgrace' and remove her from the Community, is revealed to be a weak and unreliable drunk who is easily outwitted by Isis on the rail journey south. However, the truly flawed characters in the novel, exhibiting both hypocrisy and fundamental dishonesty, are Salvador Whit and his grandson Allan, Isis' brother. Underneath his upright and diligent outward appearance, Allan is self-serving in his plans for the commercial exploitation of the Community, deceitful in his secret breaking of the rules of the Sect, and maliciously jealous of his sister Isis to the extent of organising a plot to discredit her in the eyes of the Community. Salvador, the founder of the Sect, who claimed to have had visions that redeemed him from his former life, is nevertheless revealed to be hypocritical in his sexual lusts, over-fond of drinking in secret, easily deluded by Allan and ultimately not prepared to defend his chosen successor, Isis. Thus Isis finds throughout the novel that she cannot depend on her male relations to be of much help and has actively to use her own resourcefulness and intelligence to get her out of the situations that some of them have landed her in.

Nevertheless, she is not without allies, once she is able to discover them. The respectful help she is given by the Sect's adherent in

Edinburgh, Gertie Possil, is just what she has come to expect. The continuing support, even love, that comes from the strong and sensible Sophi Woodbean arises from their long friendship. The close friendship she has enjoyed with her cousin Morag, although it is undermined and nearly destroyed by Allan's machinations, is restored in time for Morag to co-operate with Isis in her final victory. The surprise reliable friends that Isis discovers on her quest are her maternal grandmother, Yolanda Cristofiori, and her long-lost great-aunt Zhobelia. Yolanda sweeps to her aid when she is in police custody, armed with her lawyers and her money, and returns her to High Easter Offerance, perhaps corrupting her slightly with comfort and luxury in the process. And Zhobelia, discovered in the retirement home in Mauchtie, holds the key to all the mysteries surrounding Salvador and the Luskentyrian Sect. It is the female element of the plot, therefore, that sustains, rescues and resolves all Isis' difficulties. Most of all, however, it is her own female nature blending intelligence, commonsense and ingenuity that plays the major part in enabling her to win through. Isis is in the long tradition of strongminded heroines in fiction who have to make their way in a male-dominated society and assert their ability to compete on level, even superior terms, with men. Isis makes no compromises and her situation at the end is of total control within the Community.

The quest for truth

The plot of *Whit*, like that of *The Crow Road*, is patterned as a quest for the truth. The idea of the quest as a structure for a narrative goes back beyond literature and stories that are written down into the age of folk tale and fairy stories that were transmitted orally from one hearer to another through the generations. The type of story that has a hero who might be a young prince or a knight setting out on a quest to slay a dragon or rescue a princess or find the Holy Grail or discover a treasure is familiar in all ages and cultures. It tends to follow a set pattern or formula; there are dangers to be faced and overcome, with a villain or evil force to be defeated, and a successful outcome will eventually be reached.

Whit is no exception to this rule. The way that the narrative proceeds can be readily analysed into its clear components. The story begins with a brief reference to the theme to be followed up, in this case the idea of truth and self-knowledge implied in the memory of the healing of the fox by Isis. There follows an orientation to the situation and characters, the nature of Luskentyrianism and the character of Isis herself, with her

inquisitiveness, intelligence, ability to defend herself and her
naivety about the outside world.

The story then develops its first main sequence, in which a
mystery about Morag is identified and Isis is dispatched, with
various items to help her, with the mission of discovering the
truth about her cousin's apparent betrayal of the Sect. Isis has
various adventures in London and the South before she has to
admit defeat and return home with the quest apparently a failure.

The second sequence of narrative then develops, in which it
becomes clear from new evidence that the real quest is for
something else, the truth about a plot against Isis in which Allan
is deeply involved. Isis embarks upon this second quest within the
Community and then in Edinburgh and Lanarkshire where she
discovers Zhobelia and realises that there is a further dimension
to her quest, the truth about Salvador and the real origins of the
Luskentyrian Sect. This further quest takes her to Glasgow where
she uncovers the final evidence.

The successive quests are all resolved in a confrontation
between Isis the heroine and the 'villains', Allan and Salvador,
and Isis achieves final success. Yet it seems to be that the true
quest all along, unrealised by Isis, has been her quest for self-
knowledge. The mystery suggested at the beginning of the novel,
about Isis' special power, has been to some extent solved: Isis'
healing gift has come to her as an inheritance from her mother's
Eastern origins, seen also in Zhobelia's visions and intuitions
which she had passed on to Salvador for him to claim as his own.
There is also a realisation by Isis that she has the confidence and
ability to exercise power on her own behalf. Through her
experiences of having to deal with the problems of the quest, she
has, incidentally but most importantly for her own life, achieved a
degree of self-knowledge to apply in the future.

Religion and power

A central preoccupation of *Whit* is the nature of religious belief
and organisation, and how it can be used as a means of exercising
power over people's lives. Isis refers to it at the end as "action at a
distance......palpable power" (p.455). We might expect that Iain
Banks, as a self-admitted opponent of religion, which he considers
to be harmful superstition, would present a thoroughly
unfavourable picture of religion in his fiction. In *The Crow Road*,
this is generally the case, although religion does not bulk large in
the story. In *Whit*, the author's attitudes are not so clear-cut,
probably because it would not make for a good story if the main

institution of the plot were depicted as totally deluded and harmful.

Instead of using an actual church or sect as the subject of his fiction, Banks creates a religious sect specially for his narrative purpose. The Luskentyrian Sect of the Select of God is conceived as an independently existing religion with the typical apparatus of theology, scriptures, services and festivals, special rules and observances, and hierarchical organisation. The model is that of many an evangelical or fundamentalist Protestant sect; the founder, Salvador Whit, is revealed late in the novel to have been brought up by a grandmother who was a member of an extreme group, the Grimsby Brethren. Salvador is presented as a man of unknown origins, who claims to have visions from God that form the basis of his teaching and writing; he is both a Prophet and a Messiah, as his adopted name 'Salvador' (Saviour) suggests. To follow him is the way to salvation, and his disciples are the Select of God, reminding the reader of the Calvinist doctrine of the 'elect', those who are chosen by God to be saved from sin and damnation into eternal life. In addition, the Sect is like the world's great religions in having Eastern origins, not in India or Palestine or Arabia but in the shop-van of two Khalmakistani sisters in the Outer Hebrides. Salvador's writings form the first version of the Sect's bible, or holy book, the "Orthography". 'Orthography' literally means 'straight (or 'correct') writing', and generally is used to mean 'spelling'; but here there are associations with the idea of 'truth' and a 'gospel'. However, the "Orthography" is not fixed, but subject to constant revision and amendment by Salvador and Allan, just as the books and form of the Bible were constantly edited and rearranged by clergy and scholars in the early years of the Christian Church. The basis of Luskentyrianism is a particular theology, which Banks develops in Chapter Three, in which God is referred to by a singular word but identified as 'They' because "God is both and neither male and female, and everything else as well."(p.52). For somebody who is supposed to be anti-religious, Banks does an interesting and convincing job of creating an attractive-sounding doctrine for the Luskentyrian Sect. It would be of profit and interest to any students of the book to set the Luskentyrian theology alongside any other religion and discuss their relative merits.

Like many another religion, the Select of God have their own special customs and observances which set them apart from the world outside and all the Unsaved who inhabit it. Reverse-buttoning, imprinting the forehead with mud, avoiding the use of modern means of communication, using hard boards for sitting on – all these and others may seem quaint to the reader. It is clear that Banks intends the reader to take them as being of equal merit within the Luskentyrian faith as other characteristic customs are within other faiths. We can, however, suspect that Banks is being humorously playful when he gives the Luskentyrian Sect its own particular sacred substances for use in ceremonies. On the analogy of bread and wine in the Christian communion, a Luskentyrian attaches a special significance to tea-leaves and lard, since they were used by the Asis sisters to anoint the nearly-drowned Salvador; and like holy water, *zhlonjiz* (a mixture of Sloane's Liniment and herbs) has supposedly sacred properties.

Luskentyrianism, like other faiths, has its heresies, such as the Heresy of Size, which caused some of the Sect to believe, wrongly, that the larger and fatter one was, the fitter one would be to receive God's messages. Like some other sects in the history of religion, the Select of God had obtained an unwanted reputation for being sexually promiscuous, because of their Festival of Love every four years, which involved free lovemaking and much consumption of alcohol. This reputation is created by the media, but Banks is clearly mindful of the way in which different Christian groups through the centuries were persecuted by the official church using the charge of sexual immorality as one of the justifications.

Finally, the Luskentyrian Sect is presented as having a structure and organisation that reminds the reader of key aspects of other religions. Salvador is a kind of Pope, as well as being Prophet and Saviour. His original adherents, the Asis sisters, are like chosen disciples and continue as Salvador's wives to provide the top layer of the Sect's hierarchy in Salvador's children; Salvador is literally a Holy Father. There is a line of succession created through the Leapyearian offspring, Christopher and Isis, in direct line from Salvador. At a lower level, there are the first converts, and then the Sect's benefactors, and finally the general brothers and sisters of the Community, living in a kind of monastic order preserving their purity in withdrawal from the wider world. Yet, within this removed community, there are the dangers of subversion. Like much larger religious institutions, the Community is threatened by the materialistic motives of an ambitious self-seeking individual.

The parallels with other forms of organised religion are carefully and fully drawn because Banks has a larger purpose than merely satirising religion as a whole. Banks is interested in exploring the question of power and how it is exercised by controlling people at a distance through belief. A paradox of the religion presented by Banks is that, although its origins are revealed to have been rooted in a shady individual escaping the consequences of crime and in dubious visions falsely claimed by him, the Community that emerges is basically benevolent and kindly. What Isis has to resolve to herself at the end is whether the Community deserves to continue as it has done, even if based on a set of lies. Should the Truth about the religion and its founder be told to a set of devout believers? Can it continue as a more democratic institution based on the will of the community members, without the cement of faith in a doctrine and a saviour? Isis decides to tell the Truth, but we are not told the result of this revelation.

Perhaps Banks is as uncertain as the conclusion suggests. He presents religion as a sham, echoing Prentice McHoan's words in *The Crow Road*, "All the gods are false." Yet he also presents it as being capable of underpinning a worthy life and a virtuous community. The power that organised religion wields may be illegitimate, deriving its authority from either a deliberate deception or a unwitting delusion. And yet there would be a danger in its total and sudden removal in favour of a policy of telling the truth at all times, since this contains no clear guidelines for a continuing benevolent society. A sign of Banks' uncertainty may be found in the way in which *Whit* ends with the question of the reality of Isis' healing power remaining unanswered. Is Isis the possessor of a paranormal gift passed on to her from her Asian forebears? If she is, does this give her a moral or spiritual authority to continue to control the rest of the Luskentyrian Community? Isis has shown herself to be intelligent, resourceful and considerate, so that her personal qualities would fit her for exercising responsibility. From her upbringing within the Community she is also the inheritor of the respect and honour due to a Leapyearian. Thus she is well-placed to lead the Luskentyrian Sect to a more democratic and perhaps more secular continuing existence as a morally guided and self-sufficient community with an environmentally friendly life-style. *Whit* may therefore have lurking within it the blueprint for a sustainable middle way between the technologically dominated world of the Unsaved and the superstition-based life of the Select of God, a respectable haven for those unhappy with the culture and expectations of mainstream society.

Section Five
CONCLUSION

The three novels that have been considered in the preceding
sections can be regarded as strong and typical examples of Iain
Banks' work as a novelist of modern life and society. The themes
that he examines in these novels have been the concern of many
serious writers both past and present. The opposition of truth and
illusion, the conflict of parents and children, and the Scottish
dimension to these themes are central to all three novels. The
morality of scientific experimentation lurks within the plot of *The
Wasp Factory*, while the authenticity of religious belief is
examined in *The Crow Road* and *Whit*. The flawed nature of
apparently worthy and respectable members of society is revealed
in selected characters of the novels, who nevertheless are
presented as possessing a positive, even worthy, side to their
personalities. And, finally, Banks usually has something to say or
imply about male and female qualities within humanity, mostly
with a bias toward the female.

The techniques that Iain Banks uses through the whole range
of his novel output, including his science fiction, can be seen to
some degree within the three selected novels. His fondness for split
narratives, with a main 'present' narrative and a secondary 'past'
narrative alternating within single chapters, is clearly visible. In
The Crow Road, it probably reached its highest degree of
complication, producing a difficult sequence of episodes that Banks
has never tried to imitate in later writings. While the action of the
novels can be seen to be firmly located in the real present of
Scotland and Britain of the 1980s and 1990s, Banks manages to
create a specific world within this real world that contains aspects
of the surreal or almost fantastic. The action of *The Wasp Factory*
is contained within a limited area, a bleak little island which
Frank has constructed into his own fantasy world. *The Crow Road*
is centred on the 'territory' of a single family, located in a real part
of Argyll but containing unexpected features, like a glass factory, a
castle with an observatory, a mound of stones from all over the
world, and two murder scenes. *Whit* has its enclosed religious
community and its journeys by unconventional means of transport.
In the range of characters, Banks has applied a similar kind of
restriction, creating a 'family' in each novel beyond which he tends
not to range in creating main characters. We can find such
techniques being applied to the other novels he has written.

In tone and style, Iain Banks has created his own individual blend of colloquial naturalism, sensational depiction of certain kinds of event, and humorous, even playful, invention. The main narratives are always clear and convincing with their accurate realistic dialogue and straightforward presentation of the action. This tends to highlight the sensationalism and violence when it occurs, notably in *The Wasp Factory* and later novels like *Complicity* and *A Song of Stone. The Crow Road* is the most naturalistic of the three chosen novels, but in *Whit*, we can find a gentle humour being used frequently to provide a kind of comment on Isis' surprise at what she finds in the world outside the Community. Banks also indulges himself in a number of jokes within *Whit*, such as the food that has become typical of the Community, blending Scottish and Asian elements (like kipper bhoona and lorne sausage shami kebab), and his creation of the imaginary Asian country of Khalmakistan, suggesting Calmac, the ferry company running services to the Western Isles where Aasni and Zhobelia lived. Iain Banks is fond of including games, mainly invented, within his novels: in *The Wasp Factory*, Frank has his mental scenario of fantasy games and adventures; In *The Crow Road*, Prentice and Lewis have created their violent board game, the Black River Game, out of the pacifist game devised for them by their father; and in *Whit*, the whole apparatus of religious observances of the Luskentyrian Sect has the quality of a complicated game. It is a feature of Banks' writing that is particularly noticeable in his science fiction and in a book like *Complicity* or *The Bridge*, where he in fact plays a game with the reader over the unrevealed name of his main character, planting clues to the name within the text.

With such inventive variety and fertile imagination, Iain Banks remains a novelist who is full of surprises for the readers who follow his work. He can only be properly appreciated by reading a number of his books and keeping up with the changing and developing nature of his work. The three novels dealt with here can give some of the flavour of Iain Banks' writing, but the best result of reading them would be to feel inspired to read more of the work of this talented and entertaining contemporary Scottish novelist.

BIBLIOGRAPHY

Fiction published as by Iain Banks:
The Wasp Factory: Macmillan (London) Limited, 1984
Walking on Glass: Macmillan (London) Limited, 1985
The Bridge: Macmillan (London) Limited, 1986
Espedair Street: Macmillan (London) Limited, 1987
Canal Dreams: Macmillan (London) Limited, 1989
The Crow Road: Scribners, 1991
Complicity: Little, Brown and Company, 1993
Whit: Little, Brown and Company, 1995
A Song of Stone: Abacus, 1997
The Business: Little, Brown and Company, 1999

Fiction published as by Iain M. Banks (Science fiction):
Consider Phlebas: Macmillan (London) Limited, 1987
The Player of Games: Orbit, 1988
Use of Weapons: Orbit, 1990
The State of the Art (novella and short stories): Orbit, 1991
Against a Dark Background: Orbit, 1993
Feersum Endjinn: Orbit, 1994
Excession: Orbit, 1996
Inversions: Orbit, 1998
Look to Windward: Orbit, 2000

Criticism:
Thom Nairn, "Iain Banks and the Fiction Factory", *The Scottish
    Novel Since the Seventies: New Visions, Old Dreams,* Gavin
    Wallace and Randall Stevenson, eds., Edinburgh University
    Press, 1993.
Andrew Wilson, "Interview: Iain Banks", *Scottish Book Collector*,
    Vol.4, No.9, Feb.-Mar., 1995.
Alan MacGillivray, "The Worlds of Iain Banks", *Laverock*, No.2,
    1996.
Dan Coxon, "A Song of Scotland: Iain Banks as Cultural
    Ambassador", *Cencrastus*, No.62, Spring 1999.